The Luftwaffe in the Battle of Britain

The Luftwaffe in the Battle of Britain

IAN ALLAN
Publishing

Dedication
To Martine and Philip
May they never know the horrors of war

Acknowledgements
The author wishes to extend his grateful thanks for the help received while researching this book, especially to Frau Anthonie Gans and to the following: Jos Charita; AVM E. Crew; Dieter Fiechtner; Otto Franke; Adolf Galland; Christopher Goss; Walter Grabmann; Steve Hall; Gotthard Handrick; Derek Johnson; Bernard Jope; Rudolf Kratz; Helmut Meyer; Eduard Neumann; Ernst Obermaier; Willi Perchermeier; Otto Pilger; Andy Saunders; Wolf Schäfer; Kurt Sochatzy; Hannes Trautloft; Kenneth Walker; Spencer Wilson; Chris Wren; Benno Wundshammer.

Two of those who helped deserve special thanks: Jean Dillen, a specialist on everything connected with the history of Deurne-Antwerp aerodrome, who greatly assisted with the research for the chapter 'An Occupied Airfield', and last but not least Georges Van Acker, who pored over each and every photograph in this book with a magnifying glass, identifying each aircraft, looking for the odd detail and in general, greatly assisting me with writing the photo captions.

I would also like to thank the following institutions for their assistance: Bundesarchiv, Koblenz and Freiburg; Deutsche Dienststelle WASt, Berlin; Imperial War Museum, London; Lufthansa, Cologne; Ministry of Defence (Air Historical Branch and Naval History Branch), London; Volksbund Deutsche Kriegsgräberfürsorge e.V., Kassel.

First published 1980
This impression 1998

ISBN 0 7110 2576 2 (UK)
ISBN 1-55068-050-1 (Canada)

Published by Ian Allan Publishing

an imprint of Ian Allan Ltd, Terminal House, Station Approach, Shepperton, Surrey TW17 8AS.
Printed by Ian Allan Printing Ltd at its works at Coombelands in Runnymede, England.

Published in North America and Canada by Vanwell Publishing Ltd, St Catharines, Ontario.

Code: 9803/A2

Contents

Introduction

Several books have already been written about the Battle of Britain. Its history has been told many times, its conclusions drawn, its lessons explained. This book does not try to do this all over again but simply to give an impression of how some Germans experienced some moments of the battle.

During the war nobody in Germany was permitted to write freely for the general public and this is reflected in the fact that certain unusual adjectives can be found repeatedly in official texts and photograph captions. One is led to believe that every Luftwaffe unit was *siegreich* (always victorious), every crew *siegesgewohnt* (used to victory) and every action *erfolgreich* (successful). Yet I have chosen some first-hand accounts that were written and published during the war for the simple reason that they were written by men who were actually there — before the passing of time, a faltering memory, a changed philosophy or a desire either to embellish things or make them worse changed the opinions and resulted in a very different account.

When reading such texts one should be wary of the sometimes exalted tone in which they were written. Also one has to take into account that in official Germany in 1940 the war was *'frisch-fröhlich'* — a happy affair. Other people thought differently about the war, as would the Germans themselves a short while later.

Below: Some of the participating pilots stand before Oberstleutnant Walter Loebel, Geschwaderkommodore of KG30. In the middle Maj Fritz Dönch, Gruppenkommandeur I/KG30.

OPINIONS

'A country cannot be defeated by the Luftwaffe.'
Adolf Hitler speaking at a conference on 29 May 1939.

'What General Weygand called the Battle of France is now over. I expect that the Battle of Britain is about to begin.'
Winston Churchill speaking at a secret session of the House of Commons on 18 June 1940.

'The German Luftwaffe has now begun the revenge against England.'
OKW Bericht of 20 June 1940.

'I wonder if the Reichs-Marshal, as he now toured his Luftwaffe units in France (August 1940), would have been quite so cocksure of the coming victory if he had known that, in addition to his own units, we would be recipients of his signals as well.'
F. Winterbotham in his book *The Ultra Secret*, 1974.

Below: Gone were the days when, like during August 1937, a group of 20 young German pilots came to England to do some gliding on the Downs at Dunstable, Bedfordshire. This gliding camp was held under the auspices of the London Gliding Club and was the first of its kind held in Britain.

Bottom: Instead, young Englishmen, members of the RAF, were taught how to recognise German military aircraft with the aid of models.

Civilised Opening Shots

All over Germany on 17 March 1940 a familiar voice boomed through the multitude of *Volksempfänger* — the people's wireless sets. Like countless days before, the grave voice started with the stereotyped words: *'Das Oberkommando der Wehrmacht gibt bekannt'* (The OKW makes the following statement). On this day the news bulletin announced:

'As a result of recent reconnaissance flights, strong German bomber forces undertook a mission to the north-west and attacked parts of the British fleet lying at Scapa Flow in the evening hours of 16 March. During this attack three battleships and one cruiser were hit by bombs and heavily damaged. Damage to two further warships is probable. Furthermore, the airfields at Stromness, Earth-house and Kirkwall and an AA emplacement were attacked and bombed. In spite of the enemy's strong fighter and AA defences the German bombers executed their missions successfully and returned without losses.'

Scapa Flow sounded a particularly important note to German ears because it was there on 21 June 1919 that the remnants of the Imperial German Fleet — some 70 warships — scuttled itself under orders from Admiral von Reuter. From the beginning of World War II Scapa Flow was a major target for both the Luftwaffe and Kriegsmarine. On 22 September 1939, three weeks after the war began, I/KG30 was formed at Jever and became the first Luftwaffe unit to be equipped with the Junkers Ju88A. Immediately the unit turned its attention to the British Navy and was even reported to have sunk the *Ark Royal* on 26 September.

On 16 October I/KG30, stationed at Westerland-auf-Sylt, made its first sortie over the UK proper when it attacked the Firth of Forth. Minor damage was inflicted on the cruisers *Southampton* and *Edinburgh*, and the destroyer *Mohawk*. Two of the Ju88As were shot down by Spitfires of Nos 602 and 603 Squadrons. One of these bombers was that of I/KG30's commander, Hauptmann Pohle. Pohle was replaced as Gruppenkommandeur (group leader) by Hauptmann Dönch who immediately the next day led four Ju88s on an attack on Scapa Flow, during which the training battleship *Iron Duke* was damaged.

It was not only the Ju88s of I/KG30 that had an interest in the British Navy — KG26's Heinkel He111s regularly flew reconnaissance missions to the Firth of Forth and Scapa Flow and other places of interest to the Germans. On 9 February, an He111H-1 (1H+EN, W Nr 6853, of 5/KG26 based at Westerland-

Below: Only one Junkers Ju88A-1 did not make it home. This machine of I/KG30 crash landed on the Danish Island of Lolland and was set afire by its crew. The Staffel's insignia is still visible on the engine cowling. Note dive brakes beneath right wing.

auf-Sylt) on a mission to attack shipping in the Firth of Forth, was attacked and forced down by Sqn Ldr A. D. Farquhar of No 602 Squadron. The Heinkel's pilot, Unteroffizier Helmut Mayer, landed it almost undamaged on moorland near Berwick Moor. It was subsequently examined by the RAF. Another German loss came on 1 March 1940 when No 111 Squadron shot down a Heinkel He111H-2 of KG26 that had been harassing Scapa Flow.

The reaction of the German Naval Staff to the return of the British home fleet to Scapa Flow on 8 March 1940 was expressed by their demand for large scale bombings and minelaying attacks by the Luftwaffe. The first of these came at dusk on 16 March. The first warning of the raid came at 1646hrs and six minutes later an attack by 18 Ju88As of KG30 started. They came in at 2,000m and, when over the Flow, the formation split up and delivered dive bombing attacks on the *Rodney*, *Renown* and *Norfolk*, the aircraft dropping 1,000kg bombs. HMS *Norfolk* was hit on the port side of the quarterdeck abaft Y turret. The bomb passed through three decks and exploded near Y shell room, blowing a hole in the starboard side of the ship under water and starting a fire. X and Y magazines were flooded for safety and the fire was soon extinguished. The attacks on the *Rodney* and *Renown* failed but at the same time an attack was made on HMS *Iron Duke*, which was slightly damaged by three near misses.

Concurrent with this attack on the fleet, He111s of KG26 bombed shore targets. High explosive 50kg bombs and some incendiaries were dropped from 2,000m on the naval air station at Hatston, north-west of Kirkwall, without causing any damage. Another attack, also by KG26, was directed against the landing ground near Stromness, but it only succeeded in damaging some cottages at the Bridge of Waith nearby. One civilian was killed and four wounded, the first civilian air raid casualties of the war. The total Luftwaffe force was 34 aircraft, 18 Ju88s and 16 He111s, of X Fliegerkorps, though five of the He111s did not reach their objective because of mechanical trouble, which caused them to break off their mission. Apart from one Ju88 which had to belly land on the Danish island of Lolland, the Luftwaffe sustained no losses.

Above: Another Junkers Ju88A-1 of 1/KG30 was hit by AA fire and is seen here back in its hangar. On this aircraft the Staffel insignia is painted on the forward fuselage which shows shrapnel damage from an exploding anti-aircraft shell, the rings painted around the points of impact was a custom only practiced early in the war. This close-up gives a good impression of the apparent disarray in the cockpit.

Left: Sitting, from left to right, Maj Dönch, Oberleutnant Magnussen and Oberleutnant Philipps giving their press conference in the Theatersaal of the Ministry of Propaganda in Berlin.

Above right: Oberstleutnant Loebel holding a metal warship model used for reconnaissance training by the Luftwaffe; to his left Oberleutnant Philips.

Top: Hans-Werner Magnussen photographed in 1936 at Travemünde just before his first solo flight.

Above: While the participants of the raid on Scapa Flow were giving a press conference, some participants of the RAF retaliation raid against the Luftwaffe seaplane base at Hörnum on Sylt were receiving their DFCs. Photo shows Acting Flt Lt J. J. Bennett being congratulated after leaving Buckingham Palace. Bennett, a 26-year old bachelor from West Didsbury, Manchester, who took part in the raid, received the Distinguished Flying Cross for gallantry in the action when the King held an investiture at Buckingham Palace early April 1940.

The day after the attack three of the participating officers gave a press conference for the German and international Press in the *Theatersaal* of the Propaganda Ministry in Berlin. This was not an unusual practice at that time — Oberstleutnant Schumacher, Oberleutnant Steinhoff, Hauptmann Falk and Oberleutnant Pointner had already given a press conference on 19 December 1939, the day after the aerial battle over the German Bight. Thus on 17 March 1940 Hauptmann Fritz Dönch, Gruppen-kommandeur of I/KG30, Oberleutnant Magnussen, also of KG30, and Oberleutnant Philipps of KG26 spoke to the press. Hauptmann Dönch said:

'We had known for a while that the English had moved their home fleet to Scapa Flow. This brought them within our range, but we did not attack immediately, waiting for favourable weather so that the mission might have the best results. The unit had been briefed several days previously and everyone was aware of the situation. Failure was impossible and the results were better than we had anticipated. Everything went according to the book, like a parade in front of foreign dignitaries. The eagerly awaited attack took place on 16 March. After a final briefing we were on our way to Scapa Flow.

'We did not fly direct, preferring a more roundabout route. The weather was still not too good; rain and snow showers limited visibility. When we got close to Scapa Flow, however, the weather gods were kind to us and in the evening light we could see heavy ships far below. To our astonishment there were more than we had

expected. What came next was the result of our complete preparation. Everything went as expected. We had the advantage of surprise and the bombing attacks were effected with great accuracy. Several ships received direct hits, others were damaged by bombs that fell in their vicinity.

'AA fire became heavier during the attacks, apparently without results. As far as I know we received only one hit, but the aircraft was able to return to its base. The attacking British fighters did not harm us either, enabling the attack to be carried out according to plan, and by 1955hrs it was all over. From far away we could still see the light of the burning British ships.

'Flying back we were, of course, in high spirits and our reception at base was magnificent, our joy no less. Once again a successful attack had been carried out.'

Oberleutnant Magnussen had the following to say:

'The attack on Scapa Flow on 16 March was my 13th mission against England. For some time we had been waiting for an opportunity to sink some heavy ships and on the 16th we had our chance at last. Tension had reached the highest level: everything that had been discussed during the last days had now to be carried out.

'The flight to Scapa Flow went according to plan. Until the time of attack we killed time by listening to music from the stations we used as beacons and my wireless operator delighted us by playing his mouth organ. We arrived above Scapa Flow at the planned time. I had been there several times before so it was not new to me. We could see five heavy ships quite clearly — either heavy cruisers or battleships.

'All was quiet on board our aircraft now. Everybody waited for the order to attack. The bombardier was bent over his bombsight and the tension mounted. There could only be seconds to go... Then came the order to drop the bombs. The time between the order and the report of success tautened nerves to the extreme. Then came the happy shout, "They have hit". The ship I had attacked had been badly hit, the bow being engulfed in smoke and flames. How badly the ship had been damaged was proved by the smoke cloud above it which we could still see while we flew back. For some four or five minutes as I circled above the scene of the attack, we were shot at by AA guns. The fire was rather aimless and it did not trouble us. Suddenly the gunner reported "Achtung, fighters from above." I saw a single-engined fighter hurtling towards my aircraft. I circled sharply and managed to lose it.

'Now and then we glanced back at the scene of the attack and even when we were six or seven nautical miles from Scapa Flow we could still see the burning ships.'

Oberleutnant Philipps concluded:

'While the other units had been ordered to attack the warships we had observed at Scapa Flow, our targets were the airfields of Earth-house, Stromness and Kirkwall. We had to see to it that the English could not mount an effective counter-attack. After having flown different routes all our units concentrated over the Orkneys. At the southern end of Scapa Flow we saw the heavy ships, and soon the light flashes showed that the other units had done a good job. That was the scene before I attacked.

'The airfield at Earth-house was our first target. Things were not going to be too easy for us. Fighters had been reported in the area and this warned us to be cautious. Two of them tried to attack me but I dived slightly and got away from them. Calmly we dropped our bombs on the airfield. Dust and smoke clouds were soon followed by conflagrations and then we had to move on to the next target. Some fighters tried to attack us from below but they had taken off too late and we were able to get away without difficulty.

'Soon I had escaped into the darkening eastern sky. Once more we had to attack, and again we had no problems. Soon the fires glowing below proved that our mission had been completed successfully. AA fire was intense but not well aimed and not one of us received heavy damage. The Heinkel He111 had proved itself splendidly once again, over the sea and during the attack on Scapa Flow.'

Dönch, Philipps and Magnussen* were the first Luftwaffe bomber pilots whose names became known to the public in World War II.

---

*Magnussen was killed in action in Holland on 10 May 1940. Philipps was killed in action over England on 3 January 1941. Loebel was posted missing near Smolensk, Russia, on 6 September 1941 and Dönch died in a flying accident at Foggia, Italy, on 14 June 1942, having been awarded the Ritterkreuz on 19 June 1940.

The attack was widely publicised at the time, *Der Adler* of 2 April headlining *'Alarm im Hafen'* (Alarm in the harbour) while *Luftwelt* devoted nearly eight pages of its 15 April 1940 issue to the attack.

The British War Cabinet however, decided to retaliate and allowed the RAF to bomb the Luftwaffe seaplane base at Hörnum-auf-Sylt. This base was situated only 11km south of Westerland from where the German bombers had taken-off to attack Scapa Flow. It was to be the first RAF attack against a German land target and had also been chosen as it was in an isolated position so that the chances of hitting civilians would be minimal. One would be tempted to say that war was being waged in a civilised way, if such a thing was possible.

On the night of 19/20 March 30 Whitleys and 20 Hampdens attacked the seaplane base. One Whitley failed to return. No damage whatsoever was done.

The total result of the Luftwaffe and the RAF attacks was one civilian casualty and some damage to two warships. An escalation had started however that would result during the next five years in hundreds of thousands of civilian casualties and the total destruction of some of Europe's finest cities.

Below: ... and while RAF members received the DFC, the Kommodore of KG26, Oberst Robert Fuchs, was awarded the Ritterkreuz on 6 April 1940 in recognition of KG26's actions against the British Fleet during the winter of 1939/40 and against Scapa Flow on 16 March. Fuchs, a Berliner, was the fifth Luftwaffe member and the first bomber pilot to be awarded the Ritterkreuz. The photo shows him at Tempelhof aerodrome on 7 April 1940. Fuchs led KG26, the 'Löwen Geschwader' during the Battle of Britain.

Flying the Heinkel He111

As recounted in the last chapter, He111H-1 1H+EN (W Nr 6853) of 5/KG26 was shot down on 9 February 1940. It was a comparatively new aircraft, as it had been delivered to KG26 on 22 August 1939, a few days before the outbreak of World War II. On its last Luftwaffe flight it was flown by Unteroffizier Helmut Meyer while Obergefreiter Heinz Hedgemann was bombardier/gunner, Josef Sange the observer and Franz Wieners the wireless operator who was killed when Sqn Ldr A. D. Farquhar attacked the bomber. The machine ran into a stone wall, puncturing its petrol tanks, but was soon repaired and flown to the RAE whose report on the aircraft follows:

Take-off

This is quite straightforward with no tendency to swing. The initial and final climb are roughly what a pilot would expect from an aircraft of this size and power.

Below: A mission has been ordered and small trees used to camouflage this He111H-2 are taken away. Note that the glazed nose and the engines are covered over.

Approach and Landing

The most comfortable approach speed seems to be about 95mph, there being an impression of sinking at 88mph and of diving at 105mph, flaps and undercarriage down. Stalling speed is 96mph flaps up, and 83mph flaps down. When gliding at 110mph flaps up, the aileron control is rather ineffective, and it pays to use engine to assist turns. Lowering the flaps slightly improves the aileron effectiveness. At 95mph the flaps come down in 22 seconds, while raising them takes 12 seconds; little change of trim is apparent.

Landing is simple, even an indifferent landing seems good as the aeroplane is difficult to bounce. There is no tendency to swing during the ground run, which is rather long.

Taxying

The toe brakes are awkward to operate, and heavy pressure is needed on them to get the desired braking effect. As a result, taxying is difficult. View is excellent with the seat in the 'up' position.

A unique feature of the aeroplane is that the pilot is normally totally enclosed in the transparent nose. For take-off and landing he sets going a mechanism which raises both his seat and the main flying controls a foot or so upwards, his head protruding through a hole in the roof, being shielded from the airstream by a small windscreen which is erected on raising the seat.

Longitudinal Stability

Trim curves, done at two CG positions, indicate that the aeroplane has an ample static margin, of the order of 0.1C, stick fixed and free, engines off and on; this figure is applicable to the normal CG position of about 0.3C.

The elevator trimmer range appears adequate.

Above: Close-up of the Ikaria spherical mounting in the glazed nose of a Heinkel He111. It was very important to keep the extensive glazing clean in order to provide the pilot with an unobstructed view outside.

Left: RAF equipment is used by the Germans to remove the propeller of this Heinkel He111P-1.

Below left: Manhandling a SC250 is not easy — Four men are needed to lift the 250kg bomb off the ground. Note taut muscles on man at right.

Above right: Heinkel He111H-5, with glazed nose still covered and probably belonging to KG26, receives its second heavy bomb. One is already in place on the starboard PVC rack.

Right: Heinkel He111H-2 with its nose still covered by a tarpaulin. In front of it are Luftwaffe airmen awaiting their orders to start on another bombing mission. Note life-jackets worn by aircrew, a sure sign that they have to cross the English Channel.

Top right: Luftwaffe aircrew enjoying a good meal. Behind them is a Heinkel He111H-2 in its dispersal area.

Centre right: Last-minute instructions are given by a Luftwaffe Major. The aircrew are wearing the summer flying suit and their life-jackets. Note starter trolley beneath Heinkel He111P-2.

Below: Crew member boarding his Heinkel He111P-4 through the ventral gondola. Note parachute pack, briefcase and side arm, in this case a P-08 Parabellum, better known as a Luger.

Below right: Leutnant Albert von Schwerin discussing flight plan with fellow crew member. Von Schwerin received the Ritterkreuz on 31 July 1940 and was killed in action on 19 November 1940. In the background is a Heinkel He111H-3 of I/KG26.

Left: Heinkel He111H-2 starting its take-off run on an airfield in France.

Below left: Radio operator/gunner at his station in a Heinkel He111H-3. This crew member is wearing fleece-lined flying boots, summer flying suit and an unlined flying helmet. Note spare twin ammo drums for the 7.92mm MG15.

Below: Heinkel He111H-2 getting into the air.

Flight on One Engine

If one engine is throttled back when cruising level at 170mph and no corrective action is taken, the aeroplane very slowly goes into a diving spiral with the wing down about 55°. Ample control is available to recover from the spiral without opening up the dead engine.

The aeroplane can be trimmed to fly straight and level on one engine with feet and hands off. It can be flown on one engine with the rudder held central; the live engined wing must be put down about 12° for this, about half aileron being needed.

'One control' Tests, Flat Turns and Sideslips

The aeroplane was trimmed to fly straight and level at 178mph.

Ailerons fixed central

If the rudder is abruptly displaced the nose swings through about 20° before bank starts to build up. On releasing the rudder it returns to central, the aeroplane does a few oscillations in yaw, and then settles in a banked turn with the wing slowly rising.

Banked turns can be done on rudder alone, ailerons fixed. If the rudder is applied gently, entry and recovery can be made smoothly with little sideslip, while in the steady turn no sideslip is appreciable. If the rudder is released in a 30° banked turn, ailerons fixed, the wing will eventually slowly come up.

Left: Inside the cockpit of a Heinkel He111. From left to right are the navigator/bombardier, the radio operator/gunner and the pilot.

Below: Navigator/bombardier on the look-out in a Heinkel He111H-3.

Centre: High above the clouds, two Heinkel He111H-2s on their way to their target.

Bottom: Heinkel He111P-4, with additional frontal armament, flying home in company of another He111.

Rudder fixed central
Abrupt displacement of the ailerons causes appreciable opposite yaw. On release they return to central. Little oscillation of the aircraft is apparent. Good turns can be made on ailerons alone, hardly any sideslip being noticeable on entry or recovery unless the ailerons are used very harshly.

Steady flat turn
Full rudder can be applied, but very considerable foot load is needed. There is no tendency for the rudder to overbalance in the sideslip. About half opposite aileron is needed to hold the wing level. Rate of flat turn is very slow.

Steady sideslips when gliding
The maximum angle of bank in a steady sideslip at 110mph, flaps and undercarriage up is 20°. Aileron is the limiting control (an unusual feature), about quarter rudder being needed in conjunction with full opposite aileron. The aeroplane becomes slightly tail heavy. On releasing all three controls the aeroplane swings into the sideslip with the nose rising, and the wing comes up.

In a steady sideslip at 110mph with the flaps and undercarriage down, aileron is again the limiting control, about half opposite rudder being used with full aileron. The aeroplane is slightly nose heavy in the sideslip, and on releasing controls the nose drops a little, swings into the sideslip, and the wing comes up.

Control 'feel'
The controls are reasonably well harmonised at cruising speed. They become rather heavy in the dive, but show no abnormalities, and 'are about correct for this size of aeroplane'.

The Heinkel He111H-1 was allotted serial AW177 but crashed killing six of the ten passengers on board on 10 November 1943 at Polebrook while trying to avoid Ju88A-5 HM509 landing on the same runway at the opposite end.

If the Heinkel did not survive the war, its pilot Helmut Meyer did. It was not the first time that he had had to make an emergency landing with a Heinkel He111. Living in Herford in 1979, he remembered:
'In the summer of 1939, as a pilot with 5/KG26, flying Heinkel He111Bs, I took part in a large flying display at the Braunschweig-Waggum airfield. While flying at a height of only 100m my left engine stopped suddenly. I had to veer away from our formation,

Left: Could flying a He111 be so boring that the crew started to read the *Feldzeitung der Armee an Schelde, Somme, Seine*, a newspaper for German troops in the Scheldt, Somme and Seine area?

Below: After its return from a bombing mission this Heinkel He111H-3, belonging to II/KG26 'Löwen Geschwader', has its oil tank filled up by groundcrew members. Note the small retractable windscreen on top of the cockpit. If the pilot had to land his aircraft in poor weather conditions with bad visibility, he could elevate his seat and stick his head out. The small windscreen protected him against the wind and rain.

and I tried to reach the airfield. While on finals the right engine stopped as well, and I had to land on a field planted with sugar beet. Normally one makes such a landing with retracted wheels, but I simply did not have time to retract them — luckily the landing went smoothly. A few minutes later a Fieseler Storch flew over our heads only five metres off the ground. We gestured that everything was OK and then heard the loudspeakers at the airfield telling the audience that our crew was alright, and the applause from the 15,000 onlookers.'

About his last flight against England Meyer remembered:
'After the Polish Campaign, our KG26 was transferred to Westerland-auf-Sylt. We were only allowed to attack ships. Attacks against targets on land were strictly forbidden, even against AA gun sites. Our flights lasted up to 11 or 12 hours, depending upon the mission ordered. There were many dangerous moments — not only had we to cope with AA fire, Hurricanes and Spitfires, but icing was a very real danger. We could only avoid it by flying as low as possible above the water of the North Sea.

'On 9 February 1940 we were ordered to attack shipping between the Firth of Forth and Hull. We took-off around eight o'clock and arrived around 12 o'clock at the Firth of Forth. We sighted a convoy at once. Weather conditions were more favourable than ever before. Cloud base was at only 100m and it

was very foggy. None of the crew had thought it possible that we could encounter enemy fighters. But we would soon be wiser.

'During the first attack, the wireless operator reported, "Fighters from the left". At first I could not believe it as we had never seen enemy fighters in such poor weather, but one attacked us and the tracers confirmed that the wireless operator was right. We did not receive any hits and I decided to make ourselves "invisible" by climbing into the clouds. I waited half an hour there, putting my hopes on the short endurance of fighters.

'But shortly after we had left the cloud, the wireless operator again reported an enemy fighter, and immediately we were hit. The wireless operator was severely injured and the left engine started to leave a white trail, the right engine a black one. This meant a loss of fuel on the left and a loss of oil to the right. I steered towards the coast and decided to make a wheels-down landing. I had no other choice as the wounded wireless operator was lying in the ventral gondola and that was a very dangerous position.

'They were frightening moments until we landed, as it was not at all certain that we were going to reach the coast. The landing was reasonably good and the observer and I dragged the injured wireless operator 100m away to safety using the dinghy as a sledge. The mechanic stayed with the aircraft to destroy it but did not succeed, however, as the two incendiary bombs carried for that purpose did not work.

'We helped our injured comrade as best we could, and the Scotsmen who had arrived in the meantime also assisted admirably. We had to leave and were taken to the police station at Berwick. A few hours later we were brought to Edinburgh Castle where we were treated very decently. We had a first talk with an RAF major but this was interrupted. When he came back he announced that our comrade had died of his injuries. I was deeply moved and the major and I were both silent for a while. Then he offered me a whisky and soda with the friendly, fatherly words: "Relax and get over this bad news".

'Then we were taken to London for interrogation. Here too we were treated in a fair way and they were not cross with us when we didn't say anything — but I was astonished to learn how much they knew about us. By way of the POW camp at Oldham, we were taken to Canada on board the *Duchess of York* on 21 June 1940. After having been a prisoner for almost seven years I finally got back home on 21 November 1946. They were very hard years because barbed wire always is barbed wire and even a good and fair treatment cannot replace liberty.'

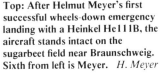

Top: After Helmut Meyer's first successful wheels-down emergency landing with a Heinkel He111B, the aircraft stands intact on the sugarbeet field near Braunschweig. Sixth from left is Meyer. *H. Meyer*

Centre: Before a mission against English shipping, from left to right: F. Sange, F. Wieners, H. Meyer and A. Siebert, all Unteroffiziere. *H. Meyer*

Above: Helmut Meyer (in the middle) helping his wireless operator Franz Wieners in to his flying suit. Wieners was wounded and later died on 9 February 1940. *H. Meyer*

Left: Meyer's He111H-1 (W Nr 6853, 1H+EN of 5/KG26 after landing on moorland near Berwick. It collided with a stone wall but damage was slight and the aircraft could be repaired.

Damage to the Englishman's Castle

While 16 March 1940 had seen the first fatal casualty in Britain as a result of a Luftwaffe attack, six weeks later, on the night of 30 April, two British civilians were killed and no less than 156 others injured when a Heinkel He111P, on a mine-laying mission in the Thames Estuary, crashed in a street at Clacton-on-Sea just before midnight. Two streets of houses were badly damaged and a whole row of homes was wrecked when two of the three parachute mines on board exploded. The first English homes, their castles, had been damaged for the first time.

The aircraft, 1T+EL, was flown by Oberleutnant Hermann-Peter Vagts (pilot), Lt Hermann Sodtmann (observer), Unteroffiziers Karl-Heinz Fresen, (flight engineer) and Hans-Günther Koch (wireless operator). They were all killed in the crash.

The He111P of KG126 had been hit by Harwich anti-aircraft guns and it started circling over Clacton-on-Sea in thick fog, on fire and with critical engine trouble. It circled the town for nearly 30 minutes, now and then firing off flares, apparently trying to find a suitable landing spot. Why the dangerous mines on board were not released over the sea remains a mystery — they might have been jammed in one way or another. Finally the pilot attempted an emergency landing resulting in the crash and explosion of two of the three mines. The aircraft carried the 1939 style and size Balkenkreuze but the heat from the fire revealed underneath those of the 1940 style and size. Probably it had been delivered from the factory in 1940 livery but when it was repainted in the field, only 1939 stencils were available. A post mortem was held on the crew and it appeared that all four had been alive at the time of the crash. They are now buried in Cannock Chase German Military Cemetery, Block 5, Row 5, graves 111 (an ironic coincidence), 112, 113 and 114.

Left: Leutnant Hermann Sodtmann, observer on board Heinkel He111 1T+EL who was killed in the crash. He was a 24-year old Leutnant from Travemünde. *via D. Johnson and S. Wilson*

This page: Three photographs showing RAF personnel examining the wreckage of the Heinkel which crashed in a street in Clacton-on-Sea.

Defeating the Defiant

No 141 Squadron had seen action in World War I and had been reformed on 4 October 1939. In early July 1940 it began Channel patrols and went into battle for the first time on Friday, 19 July 1940. It was equipped with the Boulton-Paul Defiant fighter, an aircraft that was a flying anachronism, designed to attack unescorted bombers, the result of outdated tactical theories. It also had a ghastly shortcoming: if the aircraft's electric wiring was damaged, the power-operated turret jammed and the gunner could not bale out.

On 19 July, shortly after noon, nine Defiants took-off from Hawkinge. Their mission was to patrol 20 miles south of Folkestone. They were bounced by Bf109s of III/JG51, not JG2 as is sometimes claimed. The Bf109s, led by Hauptmann Trautloft commander of III/JG51, shot down four Defiants in less than one minute. All four gunners were trapped in their turrets; none of them survived. Afterwards three more Defiants were shot down.

Herr Trautloft who fought with the Condor Legion in Spain and who after World War II became Commanding General of Luftwaffengruppe Süd of the postwar German Air Force, described the action thus:

'Just as we were sitting down to have dinner in our tent, a mission-order from the Geschwader arrived. "At 1300hrs III Gruppe will escort, with all available aircraft, a Zerstörergruppe of Bf110s, which will make a dive-bombing attack on a British freighter, equipped with AA guns, north-east of Dover."

'I had the Staffel leaders come to the Gruppe headquarters to discuss the coming mission. In the meantime Hauptmann Rubensdörffer, the commander of the Bf110 Zerstörergruppe (ErprGr210), telephoned and told he how he was going to approach and attack the target. Soon we agreed on the protection of the outward bound and return flight.

'At exactly 1300hrs, the Zerstörergruppe appeared over our airfield at St Omer. We took-off and one Jagdstaffel positioned itself to the left, one to the right and one above the Bf110s.

'Immediately after taking-off, I could see the English coast. Never before had the weather been as clear as it was that day. Until we reached the French coast we flew at 500m under scattered cloud. At the coast the cloud cover stopped and a blue sky extended ahead of us. We climbed to 3,000m and set course for the target, which we could already see from the French coast. When we got nearer, the enemy spotted us. The ship began to zig-zag at high speed.

'Exactly 18 minutes after take-off we were above our target and the Zerstörer dived on it. They dropped their bombs at 800m, pulled out of the dive and started climbing again. Then they flew home and we escorted them, shepherding them home safely.

'As we still had sufficient fuel left, I decided to do some "free hunting" with the Gruppe — the British must be somewhere; maybe they had not been alerted quickly enough and were on their way; so we headed back over the Channel again.

Right: Every Jagdgruppe had a large Abschusstafel on which every victory was carefully registered, for all to see. Here the second Abschusstafel of III/JG2 is being filled in. The shot down Defiants were mentioned on the Abschusstafel of III/JG51.

Right: Pilots of JG2 conferring with their Kommodore, Oberstleutnant Harry von Bülow-Bothkamp. Von Bülow was a World War I fighter pilot who had led Jagdstaffel 36. He had lost his two brothers in that war. On 1 April 1939, he became Inspector-General of the National Socialist Flying Corps. JG2 had no part in the attack against the Defiants on 19 July 1940 as is sometimes claimed.

Below: The Defiant's gunner had been trained in this extremely simple way to aim at attacking aircraft. This camera gun is being used by a gunner of the RAF Volunteer Reserve at a west coast depot.

'I flew with the Stabsschwarm at 3,000m. My three Staffeln were in loose formation some 1,000m higher. Visibility was so good that one could see any aircraft taking-off from the airfields near the coast. Suddenly Lt Wehnelt reported over the wireless: "Down below to the right, several aircraft just crossing the English coast." I looked towards the spot and located the aircraft, counting three, six, nine of them. They seemed to have only just taken-off. They climbed rapidly and made a large turn towards the middle of the Channel coming straight for us.

'They hadn't spotted us yet, and we headed towards them out of the sun. When I was only 800m or so above their formation I noticed the aircraft had turrets behind the cockpits. The aircraft were neither Hurricanes nor Spitfires. "Defiants", suddenly went through my head — heavily armed two-seaters whose back gunner had four heavy machine guns with enormous firepower. They had obviously been sent up to attack the bombers.

'The enemy formation was still flying tightly together, as if on exercise, when suddenly it turned back toward England. I didn't

Above: The Defiant had no chance againt the fast Bf109. Here a Bf109E-1 of I/JG77 is being taken from under its camouflaged hiding place on an airfield in France in 1940, thereby disrupting a football match under way.

Left: The remains of aircraft which the RAF had had to abandon on French airfields could be seen here and there on the airfields used by the various Jagdstaffeln — like this Gloster Gladiator being looked over curiously by Wehrmacht personnel.

Below left: The remains of this old French mill proved very convenient as an observer's platform.

understand at all what the manoeuvre was for. After checking once more for signs of Hurricanes or Spitfires, I gave the order to attack. The clock on my instrument panel stood at 1343hrs. I peeled over and dived towards the rearmost Defiant with my *Schwarmflieger*, Wehnelt, Kath and Pichon, following behind. Slightly further behind the three Staffeln followed suit. I aimed for the right hand Defiant.

'Suddenly all hell broke loose. The Englishmen had seen us. Defensive fire from a number of turrets flew towards me — fireworks all over the place. I could see the bullets passing by on either side and felt hits on my machine, but pressed home my attack. 200m, 100m — now was the time to fire and my machine guns and cannon hammered away. The first volley was too high, but the second was right in the middle of the fuselage and parts of the Defiant broke loose and flashed past me. I saw a thin smoke trail appear below the fuselage and suddenly the aircraft exploded in a huge red ball of flames which fell towards the sea.

'I'd gained speed in my dive and used it to curve into the attack again to the right. While in the turn I saw another Defiant going down behind me and to my left. By this time all my pilots were attacking, and then suddenly my engine vibrated and began to run unevenly. I could smell burning oil in the cockpit and my coolant temperature indicated 120° with the oil temperature also rising steadily. For the first time I noticed several hits on my left wing and a trail of smoke beneath it. I felt uneasy — I didn't want to have to bale out in the middle of the Channel.

'Then Kath appeared on my left. His aircraft was also trailing smoke. "I've got to make an emergency landing," he told me over the WT, and, like me, headed towards the French coast.

'It's a damned uneasy feeling flying so slowly over the sea in a shot up crate, all the more worrying when one's flying height was diminishing steadily — and all the while the coast didn't seem to be getting any closer. Luckily there weren't any enemy fighters around or we'd have been easy meat.

'At last there was land below us and I scraped over Cap Blanc Nez at 200m, finally landing at the airstrip of St Inglevert with my prop feathered. I didn't know where Kath had gone — I'd had my hands full during the forced landing and hadn't been able to follow his progress. During the flight back I'd heard the voices of my pilots over the WT, "I'm attacking" ... "Abschuss", and then I'd heard, "Achtung, Spitfires". It was obvious from that that English fighters had joined in the battle.

'After landing I got out of my aircraft as soon as possible — I could still smell burning oil and didn't want to be inside if the aeroplane exploded. Only after I'd got out could I see that my radiator had been shot to pieces.

'A young leutnant from a nearby Flak battery came towards me and asked if I was OK. He had followed the whole combat through his field glasses and told me that he had seen several aircraft going down and two parachutes. He'd also seen a German Air/Sea rescue aircraft take-off from Boulogne to pick up the pilots who had ditched and had followed the track of another aeroplane that had disappeared behind a hill near the coast, only a few kilometres from where we stood. It had been trailing smoke and was obviously making a forced landing.

'It could only have been Kath.

'I got into a truck — nothing else could be found by way of transport — and drove in the direction he had indicated. From the vantage point of a small hill I surveyed the countryside and spotted Kath's aircraft which had landed intact in a shallow valley. Soon he stood in front of me and told me how he'd shot down a Defiant and the circumstances of his own landing — his aircraft had been damaged in almost identical fashion to my own.

'I flew back to St Omer in a small Bücker aircraft and was warmly greeted. Just after I'd landed a telephone call came through from the Geschwader — another escort mission with all available aircraft for a Zerstörergruppe going to attack Dover Harbour ...'

Top: Major Gotthard Handrick, Geschwaderkommodore of JG26, preparing to take-off in a Bf109E-4. Like many Luftwaffe Battle of Britain pilots, Handrick was a Condor Legion veteran.

Above: The Stabsschwarm of III/JG51 which led the attack against the Defiants. From left to right: Oblt Kath, the adjutant, Oblt Pichon, the Technical officer, Oblt Wehnelt, the Transmissions officer Hauptmann Trautloft, Kommandeur of III/JG51. This photograph was taken at St Omer airfield from where JG51 operated at the time of the attack against the Defiants. These four pilots survived the war and are enjoying good health at the time this book was written. Herr Trautloft believes that this is the only Schwarm who survived the war. *via H. Trautloft*

Left: Major Hannes Trautloft as Kommodore of JG54 Grünherz. Until 25 August 1940 he was Kommandeur of III/JG51 and as such led the attack against the Defiants on 19 July. This photo was taken by Willhelm Reimers of Luftwaffe Kriegsberichterkompanie (mot).

Below: Hauptmann Trautloft at St Omer airfield, surrounded by some members of his III/JG51 and three RAF men, the crew of a shot down Blenheim. *via H. Trautloft*

Mölders Molested

On 19 July 1940, Werner Mölders was promoted to Major and on 27 July was appointed Geschwaderkommodore of JG51. His nickname *Vati* (Daddy) was known throughout the Luftwaffe. He was a seasoned fighter pilot who had already obtained 14 victories in Spain, and was the first Luftwaffe pilot to be credited with 20 victories and to obtain the Ritterkreuz. As soon as he received command of his Geschwader he was briefed by General Osterkamp, Jagdfliegerführer of Luftflotte 2 and on 28 July fought for the first time above English soil. That first fight almost ended in disaster.

Mölders led four Staffeln from I and II Gruppen of JG51 when they were attacked by 12 Spitfires of No 74 Squadron led by Flt Lt 'Sailor' Malan. Malan himself scored some hits on Mölder's Messerschmitt Bf109E-3. Soon after the fight Mölders wrote:

'My first flight against England will remain in my memory forever. I was flying with my adjutant, Oberleutnant Kircheiss. North of Dover we saw three Spitfires below us and more machines appeared out of the mist. We attacked the first three and I shot down one of them. However, by this time I was flying in the middle of eight or ten Englishmen and they seemed to be mad at me. They all dived towards me and that was my lucky break. Endeavouring

Below left: Major Werner Mölders, Geschwaderkommodore of JG51 waving at a returning pilot of his Geschwader.

Below: Mölders and Galland, two Geschwaderkommodores. They are still considered as the Luftwaffe fighter pilots par excellence. Galland is using the time honoured method to describe a combat — both hands.

Left: The tail of Mölders' Bf109E, W Nr 2804, shows 28 victories on 28 August 1940.

Below: Three days later, on 31 August 1940, the rudder of Mölders' Bf109E shows a total of 32 victories.

Centre: One of Mölders' pilots, Leutnant Hermann Staiger of III/JG51, lifting a bottle of Champagne for all to see after one of his victories. The gentleman sitting on top of the cockpit seems to have had his sip already. The aircraft is a Bf109E-4. *via Obermaier*

Bottom: At the end of August 1940, I/JG77 was added to Mölders' JG51 and became IV/JG51. The number 13 does not seem to have brought luck to this Bf109E-5 of IV/JG51 which had to crash land. The machine carried an unusual Blitz (lightning) embellishment. *via W. Schäfer*

to gain laurels at the expense of the solitary German, each hindered the other. I flew about furiously and confused them even more. By then it was only a matter of time before I was hit. My machine rattled wildly. The radiator and the fuel tank were damaged and all I could do was to dive away towards the Channel at 700km/h. The whole gang followed me like a waterfall. Oberleutnant Leppl had seen what was happening and succeeded in shooting down the Spitfire that was nearest to me. The pressure was off.

'Luckily the engine kept going until I reached the French coast. Then it began spluttering. When I wanted to land, the undercarriage would not lower; I had to land with it retracted — which I managed successfully. When I wanted to clamber out of the machine my legs felt singularly weak. Examining them I saw large bloodstains. My visit to hospital proved that I had three splinters in my upper thigh, one in my knee joint and one in my left foot. In the heat of the battle I had not felt a thing — the splinter in my kneecap is still there. On this occasion I experienced the fatherly solicitude of our Reichsmarschall once more; he had me flown to the *Luftwaffenlazaret* (air force hospital) in Berlin. The 11 days at the *Lazaret* were a wonderful convalescence. I believe I was something of the "showpiece" of the hospital and the sisters looked after me in a way that my own mother could not have bettered. Later on I sent the good people a sack of coffee.'

So Mölders succeeded in crash-landing his Bf109E-3 at his airfield at Wissant. Another pilot of the Geschwader, Hauptmann Erwin Aichele a Staffelkapitän of I/JG51, was not so lucky. He was hit by Freeborn of No 74 Squadron who, like Malan, was flying a Spitfire. Aichele was wounded but managed to get back to Wissant; he crashed to his death while attempting to land.

He was a well-known sports pilot who, in the 1920s and 1930s, had frequently taken part in European sports flying events. In February 1933 he married Fedie Riegele, the daughter of a well-to-do brewer of Augsburg. For his honeymoon he made a 13,000km flight around the Mediterranean in his private BFW M23b D-2142, a two-seater with open cockpits. The propeller of his Bf109E-3 was placed as a cross on his grave at Wissant.

In the summer of 1941 Mölders became the first General der Jagdflieger of the Luftwaffe. He was only 28 years old, but he died in a flying accident on 22 November 1941.

Flying the Junkers Ju88

The RAF got its first chance to examine a Junkers Ju88 in flight on 28 July 1940, when the direction-finding equipment of 9K+HL, a Ju88A-1 of 3/KG51 (WNr 7036), failed. The pilot, Oberfeldwebel Josef Bier, lost his way and landed north of Bexhill, the Ju88 being undamaged. It received the British registration AX919 and was test-flown by RAE pilots. About the Ju88 they had the following to say:

The aeroplane has a number of interesting mechanical devices designed to assist the pilot in his handling of the aeroplane.

i   The flaps may be lowered to two positions, roughly 25° for take-off and 50° for landing. With flaps up a small movable plate covers the slot gap on the wing under surface, thereby reducing drag. During the first 15° of the flap movement this plate is moved upwards, thereby opening the slot.

ii On lowering the flaps through their first 25° the ailerons are both drooped about 15° in order to increase C_1 max.

iii On lowering the flaps fully, the tailplane incidence is automatically decreased by 5° in order to counteract the change of trim and to help in getting the tail down on landing.

iv On lowering the dive brakes the elevator trimming tab is automatically moved up to counteract change of trim.
Pull-out from a steep dive during dive-bombing is automatic.

vi The rudder is fitted with a spring tab to assist in handling the aeroplane on one engine. The tab comes into action when the pilot's foot load exceeds about 30lb. The same tab is used for trimming.

vii The aileron forces are reduced at large aileron displacements by swinging weights in the wing tips.

Take-off and Landing

Take-off

The aeroplane must be taxied straight just before opening up the throttles in order to lock the tail wheel in the correct fore and aft position. Provided the throttles are opened up slowly and evenly, the tendency to swing is not very marked, while above 50mph the rudder becomes very effective. The aeroplane does not readily fly itself off, the control column having to be pulled back firmly to unstick. Take-off run is rather long, but speed builds up rapidly once off the ground, giving full control in a short space of time. The initial rate of climb is moderate. 25° flap was used for the take-off.

Approach

The undercarriage should be lowered at about 2,000ft. At the appropriate time the flap lever is moved into the first position from neutral. This half lowers the flaps and droops the ailerons; change of trim is small. During the final stage of the approach the flap lever is brought to the second position. This brings the flaps fully down and decreases the tailplane incidence, necessitating a push on the control column.

Below: The glazed nose of a Junkers Ju88A-6. Note the attachment points for the balloon cable fenders at each side of the cockpit, top and bottom. The whole contraption made the A-6 extremely vulnerable to fighter attacks and the device was removed after a few operations because of its limited success. Aircraft of this type then reverted to the bomber role as can be seen by the external bomb racks.

A certain amount of engine is normally used during the approach. If the engines are throttled right back the best approach speed is about 115mph; at 105mph there is a sensation of sinking, and at 125mph one of diving. Stalling speed flaps down is 93mph, and 116mph with flaps up. On lowering the flaps, control in general feels more 'sloppy', but is quite adequate on the glide.

Landing

The aeroplane is not easy to land. It is very difficult to get the tail fully down, the brakes must be used with caution after a wheel landing, while there is a tendency to swing after touch-down which must be immediately corrected.

Baulked Landing

The engines can be opened up fully with flaps and undercarriage down, and the aeroplane climbed away without undue difficulty. The undercarriage comes up in about 12 seconds. On raising the flaps, which come up in about 10 seconds, there is a marked sink, the nose drops rapidly and the speed increases quickly. A hard pull on the stick is needed to keep the nose up, and in the interests of safety the flaps should not be raised below about 1,000ft.

Taxying

The aeroplane handles well on the ground. Care must be taken to see that the tail wheel is unlocked (as a safety feature, to prevent retraction of the tail wheel when skew, the hydraulics are automatically put out of action unless the tail wheel is locked central). The brakes are particularly effective.

Longitudinal Stability

The centre of gravity limits are from 2.48 to 3.55ft aft of the root leading edge; since the aerodynamic chord is 9.18ft, this gives a CG range of about $11\frac{1}{2}$% of the mean chord. Trim curves at two CG

positions suggest that even with CG aft the aeroplane has a large static margin in hand, stick fixed and stick free, of the order of 0.1C on the glide and slightly less at full throttle.

Flight on One Engine

If one engine is suddenly throttled back when cruising level at 220mph and no corrective action is taken, the aeroplane banks fairly sharply and loses height, speed building up rapidly. Recovery is very easy owing to the lightness and effectiveness of the ailerons. The aeroplane can be trimmed to fly straight and level with feet and hands off, about quarter rudder being necessary.

Behaviour on throttling back one engine during a climb at 150mph is far more violent, and unless prompt corrective action is taken to prevent the wing dropping, over 1,000ft may well be lost. Provided the ailerons and rudder are applied promptly, however, correction is quite easy and there is no necessity to throttle back the live engine to retain control. Enough rudder tab is available to trim when climbing on one engine.

Recovery is rather more difficult if the flaps are set in the take-off position when climbing, as the ailerons are heavier and the manoeuvre somewhat more violent. During all these engine cutting tests with virtues of the light spring tab rudder and the light ailerons were very apparent.

Landing with one engine dead is rather precarious, owing to the violent swing and bank accompanying opening up the good engine when correcting the flight path at very low airspeeds.

'One control' Tests, Flat Turns and Sideslips

The aeroplane was trimmed to fly straight and level at 180mph, 10,000ft.

Ailerons fixed central

On suddenly applying the rudder, swing and bank build up rapidly. The rudder returns to central sharply on release, and after a few oscillations in yaw and roll the aeroplane settles in a banked turn.

Good banked turns can be done on rudder alone, the aeroplane banking unusually quickly in response to rudder movement.

Rudder fixed central

The ailerons can be applied violently without appreciable opposite yaw. On releasing the stick it oscillates from side to side a few times before returning to central. The aeroplane does a few oscillations in roll before settling down after release of the stick.

Excellent banked turns can be done on ailerons alone, with little sideslip in entry or recovery.

Steady flat turns

Full rudder can be applied, although considerable force is needed to get it fully on. About $\frac{3}{4}$ opposite aileron is required to hold the wings level. Rate of flat turn is roughly 120deg/min. There is no pronounced nose-heaviness.

Steady sideslips when gliding

Gliding at low speeds with flaps and undercarriage up the maximum angle of bank in a straight sideslip is about 30°, obtained with full rudder and $\frac{3}{4}$ opposite aileron. There is little nose-heaviness. Behaviour is the same with flaps and undercarriage down, except that there is slightly more nose-heaviness. In both cases the wing comes up rapidly on releasing all three controls, and the aeroplane quickly settles in a straight glide or a shallow turn.

Stalling Behaviour

Behaviour in a straight stall with the engines throttled back is fairly mild, flaps up or down. With flaps up the control effectiveness decreases progressively as the stall is approached, and at the stall the nose drops abruptly with little tendency for a wing to go down viciously. With flaps down more warning is given, since the loss of control effectiveness is more marked, and a buffeting is felt on the elevator at 96mph, some 3mph before the stall.

Flying Controls

Ailerons

Aileron control is excellent. Response is adequate at low speeds and for dealing with a sudden engine cut, while at high speeds the stick

Top left: A Ju88 pilot, in this case Feldwebel Otto Eichloff of 4/KG30 who was awarded the Ritterkreuz on 16 August 1940. In April he had damaged a British Navy cruiser off the coast of Norway and shortly after sank one. In the Moldefjord he had sunk a 4,000-ton steamship and, in the mouth of the River Maas in Holland, a transport ship. He had also destroyed barracks near 's Gravenhage in Holland. His crew consisted of Unteroffiziere Dehnbostel, Sänger and Röstel.

Centre left: A Ju88 crew about to board their aircraft.

Bottom left: Four Junkers Ju88As screaming down towards their targets — a spine-chilling sight.

Below centre: A Ju88 crew: Oberleutnant Gerhard Richter and his crew. Richter was Staffelkapitän of 8/LG1 and was awarded the Ritterkreuz on 24 November 1940. He had made over 100 sorties in Spain as a Condor Legion pilot.

Below: The Ju88s did not always return without damage, as proved by this Feldwebel poking his head through a hole in a Ju88A's elevator.

forces are extremely light. At 300mph more than $\frac{3}{4}$ aileron can easily be applied with one hand. At 240mph the time between the initiation of the stick movement and the stage at which the aeroplane reached 45° bank in a steady roll was measured, when the pilot applied nearly full aileron vigorously. The surprisingly low figure of 0.7 seconds to 45° bank was recorded. This places the Ju88 quite out of the common run of bombers as regards aileron performance at high speeds. The feature is, of course, of the utmost value in avoiding action.

This lightness of aileron control springs partly from aerodynamic balance and low stick gearing, and partly from an ingenious mechanical device for lightening the ailerons at large displacements. A full description and discussion of this device will be found in Appendix I. Briefly, swinging weights mechanically geared to the ailerons are mounted inside each wing tip in such a manner that when the aeroplane rolls, the centrifugal force on the weights generates a relieving hinge moment proportional to the cube of the aileron angle. Such a device can be arranged to very appreciably relieve the pilot's effort during violent manoeuvres.

Elevator

The elevator control would be inadequate for landing were it not for the automatic coupling of tailplane and flaps which decreases the tailplane incidence 5° on lowering the flaps fully. Even so there is barely sufficient elevator control for getting the tail down on landing with the CG forward.

The elevator is pleasantly light and effective at all speeds. At 250mph a normal acceleration of 4g can be put on by pulling fairly hard, without assistance from the tabs. Vigorous avoiding action is thus possible.

Rudder

The rudder is considerably lighter than is usual on aeroplanes of this size, owing to the spring tab mechanism. This is a very good feature from the viewpoint of engine cutting and evasive action. The rudder, although still light, is not over-sensitive in the dive.

Dive brakes

The procedure for dive-bombing with dive brakes out and automatic pull-out is interesting. Before entering the dive a contacting altimeter, which sounds a horn at any selected altitude, is set for the height at which the bombs are to be released; and the bomb distributor is adjusted with the assistance of standardised tables. The elevator trimmer is then set to a fixed mark which trims the aeroplane nose-heavy, and the dive is started. As the speed builds up the dive brake lever is operated and the engines throttled back.

Operation of the dive brake lever lowers the dive brakes and at the same time moves the elevator trimming tab up through 2.5°. This moves the elevator down, and causes the aeroplane to drop its nose rapidly. When a pilot first goes through the routine he finds this part of the operation quite alarming, since the aeroplane appears to bunt suddenly, with appreciable negative 'g' for a short period.

However, the tab settings are so adjusted that the aeroplane automatically trims itself in a roughly 50° dive, during which the speed builds up to about 310mph after a height loss of 6,000ft. During this period the pilot can judge his dive angle approximately by means of inclined lines painted on one of the transparent cockpit panels. He concentrates on getting his sights on the target in a steady dive at the selected angle.

When the pre-set height is approached the contacting altimeter sets a horn going. On reaching the selected height the horn noise suddenly stops. The pilot immediately presses the bomb release button.

The $2\frac{1}{2}$° up tab movement obtained on lowering the dive brakes compresses a spring in the tab circuit. The spring is tripped, via a solenoid device, on pressing the bomb release button, and the elevator tab is thereby abruptly jerked back $2\frac{1}{2}$° down. This moves the elevator up, and pulls the aeroplane out of the dive with a normal acceleration of about $3\frac{1}{2}$g.

During the pull-out, at a pre-selected time after the bomb release button which initiatates the pull-out has been pressed, the first bomb is automatically released. The whole purpose of releasing the bomb during the pull-out is, of course, to compensate for the curved trajectory of the falling bomb. The German technicians have attempted to make the process as definite as possible by reducing the possibility of piloting errors.

The pilot is not restricted to a 50° dive; any angle in the range 30° to 70° may be used. Provision is also made for use of the automatic pull-out device with dive brakes retracted for steep dive-bombing from very low altitudes.

Violent Evasive Action

A few brief tests were made as a basis for calculating the probable flight paths of the Ju88 if the pilot took various violent evasive actions after releasing his bombs.

The first point to be determined in such action is the time taken to achieve a steady bank of 60° or more by applying aileron quickly and them almost immediately holding it off to keep the bank steady; the second point is the maximum g that can conveniently be applied as soon as the bank is on. The following results were obtained at 1,500ft, all-up weight 22,000lb:

Speed (EAS) mph	Angle of bank	Time to achieve steady bank, secs	Steady g in the turn	Speed after turn through 360° mph
250	70°-80°	2.0	3.5	230
200	70°-80°	2.0	2.75	185
150	60°-65°	1.5	2.0	140

The characteristics of violent 'zooms' done by pulling the stick back vigorously when flying straight and level were next examined at 1,000ft, with the following results:

Speed (EAS) mph	Maximum g in the 'zoom'	Time to reach maximum g secs	Time to gain 100ft secs	Speed after given height gain
250	4	1.5	2.0	230mph after 150ft gain
200	3	1.0	2.0	165mph after 200ft gain

The Ju88 is obviously an extremely useful military machine, with good performance and load-carrying qualities and excellent manoeuvrability for its size at high speeds. In spite of all the refinements provided by the designer to improve the trim and control characteristics, it is however, not an easy aeroplane to operate, mainly owing to its high loading; inexperienced pilots must in particular take some time to get used to the approach and landing, especially with one engine dead. Its reputation as a somewhat 'tricky' aeroplane may be clearly discerned from the following quotation, taken from an official German handbook:

'Because of its special purposes as bomber and dive-bomber, the type Ju88 had to follow constructional principles which show several changes from what was normal hitherto.

'If the pilot bears this carefully in mind, the Ju88 presents no special difficulty; on the contrary, the pilot, after gaining experience, feels very comfortable even under difficult conditions and is enthusiastic about the fighting power of his aircraft.'

Seenot
Air~Sea Rescue

To rescue the crews of both German and British aircraft, that had come down in the sea, the Luftwaffe usually used Heinkel He59 float-biplanes. Initially these aircraft were painted white all over, carried a large red cross and civilian registration. On 1 July 1940 such an ambulance was shot down for the first time and after a short while these aircraft were camouflaged and received Luftwaffe registrations. The following Luftwaffe Seenot aircraft were lost (100%) during the second half of 1940:

Below: A Luftwaffe airman who came down in the Channel, is picked up by D-A+GUI, a Heinkel He59C-2.

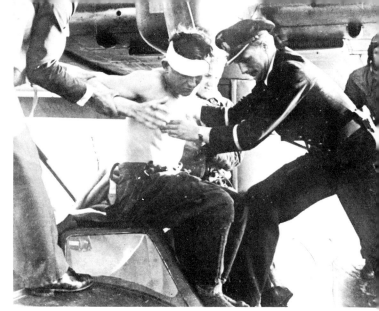

Date (1940)	Type	Unit	W Nr	Registration	Remarks
1.7	He59	Seenotflug-Kommando (SK)3		D-ASAM	Shot down by Spitfires of No 72 Sqn
9.7	He59	SK1		D-ASUO	Shot down by Spitfire of No 54 Sqn
11.7	He59	SK1			Shot down by British fighters
20.7	He59	SK1		D-AKAR	Shot down by Hurricanes of No 601 Sqn
20.7	He59	SK4			Shot down by Hurricane of No 238 Sqn
25.7	He59	SK5			Accident at Norderney
27.7	He59	SK3			Shot down by Hurricanes of No 615 Sqn
28.7	He59	SK1			Shot down by Hurricanes of No 111 Sqn
28.7	He59	SK3			Shot down by Hurricanes of No 111 Sqn
1.8	He59	Seenotzentrale (SZ) Cherbourg			Forced landing after accident
8.8	He59	SZ Cherbourg			Shot down by Hurricane of No 238 Sqn
11.8	He59	SZ Cherbourg			Shot down by Hurricane of No 610 Sqn
11.8	He59	SZ Cherbourg			Shot down by Blenheim of No 604 Sqn
12.8	He59	SK3			Accident
15.8	He59	SK4			Shot down by Spitfires of No 260 Sqn
16.8	Do24	An unknown Seenotflug-Kommando			Sea landing accident
19.8	He59	SK2			Accident at Berger
23.8	He59	SZ Boulogne	2792		Enemy action
23.8	He59	SZ Boulogne	2596		Enemy action
26.8	He59	SK2	0935		Shot down by Spitfires of No 602 Sqn
28.8	He59	SK3	1528		Shot down by Hurricanes of No 79 Sqn
28.8	He59	SK3	1512		Shot down by Hurricane of No 79 Sqn
7.9	He59	SK3	0840	DA+WT	Sea landing accident
13.9	He59	SK3	0932	TV+HM	Enemy action
14.9	He59	SK3	1513	TV+HO	Forced landing after accident
15.9	He59	SK2	0529	DA+MG	Forced landing after accident
23.9	He59	SZ Boulogne	2596		
23.9	He59	SZ Boulogne	2792		Collision
2.10	He59	SK4	1510	NO+FU	Landing in minefield
4.10	He59	SK4	2602	NE+UX	Capsized after forced landing
8.10	He59	SK2	0534	TW+HH	Shot down by Blenheims of No 235 Sqn
8.10	He59	SK2	0541	DA+MJ	Shot down by Blenheim of No 235 Sqn
26.10	He59	SK3	1984		Shot down by Hurricanes of No 229 Sqn
28.10	Do24	SK1	075		Crashed after engine failure
6.11	Br521 'Bizerte'	SK1	011	SG+FM	Enemy action
11.11	He59	SK3	1991	NE+TD	Enemy action
14.11	He59	SK3	1852		Destroyed through bad weather
14.11	He59	SK3	2862		Destroyed through bad weather
17.11	He59	SK5	1844	DS+KD	Enemy action
26.11	He59	SK3	0539	NO+FT	Enemy action

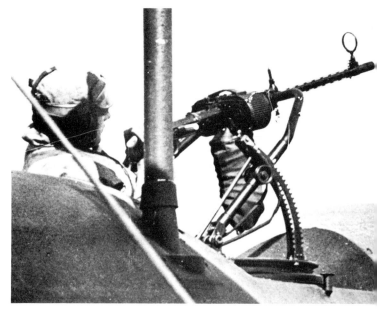

What it felt like to have to ditch into the Channel and to be rescued by an aircraft is recounted by an Oberleutnant of ZG26 who had to ditch his Messerschmitt Bf110:

'It was a formidable experience. A white trail of smoke marked the downward path of a Hurricane that we had raked with our machine

Top left: Dornier Do18s were also used for Air/Sea Rescue missions.

Centre left: After RAF aircraft had attacked the unarmed, white-painted Heinkel He59C-2 Seenotflugzeuge, the latter were camouflaged and armament reintroduced in the manner shown on this close-up of the dorsal 7.92mm MG15 position of a Heinkel He59B-2.

Bottom left: A Heinkel He59B-2 approaching a downed airman. Clearly visible is the 7.92mm MG15 on its ring mounting in the open nose position.

Above: This Heinkel He59B-2 provided the Kriegsberichter, operating with a telephoto lens, with a suitable subject. The backdrop is formed by the English coast.

Centre right: Several captured French Breguet Bizertes were used by the Luftwaffe for air/sea rescue missions. Here a Luftwaffe crew is leaving one of the three-engined biplanes.

Bottom right: This Gefreiter is operating a wireless set inside a Luftwaffe Seenot aircraft. On his left sleeve he is wearing the Luftwaffe speciality badge. This badge was worn by all flying personnel except pilot, observer and wireless operator/flight engineer. This Gefreiter is also a qualified wireless operator but lacks the mechanic qualification.

guns. But now English fighters were climbing upwards to intercept the German bomber group which was steering a course towards an airfield south of London. The bombers, however, were able to continue on their way unmolested as German fighters attacked the enemy aircraft like a pack of ravenous wolves. Thwarted by our Messerschmitts the disappointed Spitfire and Hurricane pilots wanted to obtain at least one visible result and the last German aircraft, our Messerschmitt Bf110, became the objective for the British aircraft.

'The enemy surrounded us on every side and we saw gun flashes to right and left. We shot at the enemy whenever possible but they were too many. Their bullets cracked and banged in our fuselage. The dinghy was already shot to ribbons. This could not go on any longer; we began to lose height. To bale out would mean captivity. If only we could reach the Channel!

'As if our aircraft had guessed my thoughts, the left engine suddenly came to life. The altimeter remained about zero, but, all alone jumping from cloud to cloud, the Messerschmitt Bf110 flew home above enemy territory at some 230km/h. And there, at last, the sea glistened, the last hurdle. But this hurdle was to be our destiny. Shortly before the coast that would have saved us, an accident happened. The engine conked out. Our machine dived down towards the water.

'Canopy away! We threw away the canopy and were surrounded by fire, then suddenly by water, unbelievable amounts of water. I don't know what happened exactly, anyway we succeeded in getting free from the machine; maybe we were thrown out, maybe the water snatched us from our seats. It lasted only a few seconds, which I cannot describe, then we were swimming in the Channel, both of us side by side near the French coast which was only some 500m away.

'But now disaster threatened. An upward glance showed how the sinking aircraft's stabiliser was slowly coming towards us. Swim for heaven's sake, swim ... We took off our flying boots and then, with a few heavy puffs, our life jackets inflated. They supported us while the machine sank. But the coast was still some way off and the water was cold and the current was carrying us away from land. My wireless operator had a good idea — he fired a flare from his Very pistol. That saved us. German fighters saw us in the water and four Messerschmitts circled above us. Despite the cold, the wireless operator and I smiled at each other — even if we were exhausted and injured. The fighters signalled a Seenotmaschine which came and took us aboard a short time later.'

Below: A number of *Rettungsbojen Generalluftzeugmeister* **before being anchored off the French coast. These rescue buoys which were known to the RAF as 'lobster-pots' contained four bunks with bedding and everything downed airmen might need. They served little purpose as they often broke loose. A diagrammatic drawing of such a rescue buoy was published in the** *Illustrated London News* **for 7 December 1940 and reproduced, with its English text, in** *Der Adler* **for 18 February 1942.**

Reporting the Battle

Throughout the Battle of Britain, the Germans and the peoples of the occupied countries were supplied with a barrage of articles, features, photographs and newsreels about the war in the air. The information was of an amazing quality even if always one-sided — like any information in any belligerent country.

Who wrote these texts, who took the photographs, who made the films?

The people responsible were the PK men, later named *Kriegsberichter* (war correspondents). The *Propaganda-Kompanie*, in short PK, was a unique military formation during World War II. Made up of former journalists, photographers, wireless reporters and camera operators, one could also find former poets, authors, playwrights, cartoonists, printers and so on — civilians turned war correspondents.

When the war broke out four *Luftwaffe-Propagandakompanien* (LwPK) were set up, one for each Luftflotte:

LwPK 1 in Bernau near Berlin
LwPK 2 in Braunschweig
LwPK 3 in Munich
LwPK 4 in Vienna

During 1940 these units were renamed as *Luftwaffenkriegsberichterkompanien* (LwKBK Luftwaffe War Correspondence Company) and also in 1940 four more such companies were set up:

LwKBK 5 in Jüterbog
LwKBK 6 in Dresden-Loschwitz
LwKBK 7 in Berlin-Adlershof
LwKBK 8 in Berlin-Reinickendorf

The task of the PK men or Kriegsberichter was to accompany the troops into action to report on their experiences and about the fighting in general. They often operated as a pair, one reporting in writing, the other by photograph or film. An LwKBK had an approximate strength of about 120. They were excellently equipped and had their own transportation and courier aircraft.

At the start of World War II pilots in general refused to take PK men on board for actual missions as they did not want any spectators. To get over this, on Goebbels' orders, Luftwaffe PK men were then trained as gunners and bomb aimers. During the Battle of Britain Kriegsberichter very often flew above England, not only reporting on the battle but actually taking part in it behind a machine gun. The first man from a PK unit to be decorated for his

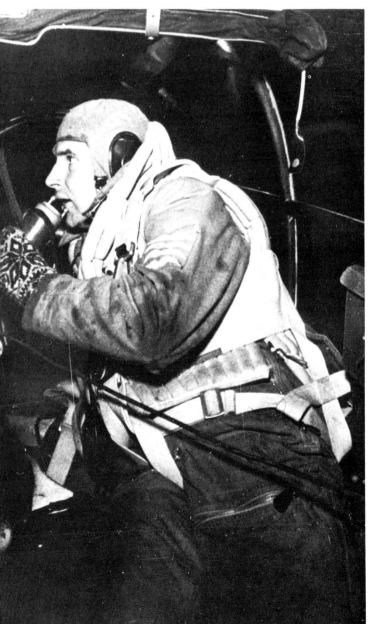

Left: A radio reporter reporting at night from a Heinkel He111 over London.

actions during the Battle of Britain was Hans Kriegler, who received the Iron Cross, Second Class.

Many Kriegsberichter were killed in action and at one time nearly a third of all the personnel of the five LwKBKs that reported on the Battle of Britain had been killed or taken prisoner. All material, text, photos, film and drawings had to be submitted first to a military censorship by the *Oberkommando der Wehrmacht* (OKW) and then to the political censorship of Goebbels'

Reichsministerium für Volksaufklärung und Propaganda (Reich's Ministry for the People's Enlightenment and Propaganda).

In 1978, one of the best known Kriegsberichter, Benno Wundshammer, remembered:

'The "fighters at home" — who of course wanted to stay in the Heimat — wrote heroic and often rabble-rousing captions for our pictures. And we Kriegsberichter at the front were scolded for it by the troops.'

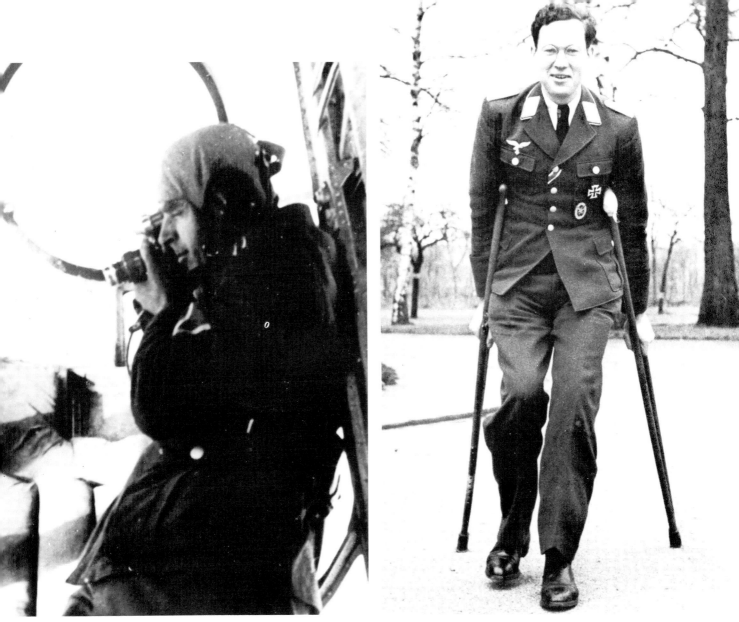

Above left: A group of cameramen is greeted by the Staffelkapitän in front of a Heinkel He111.

Left: A film camera, operated from inside the cockpit, is mounted on the left wing of a Junkers Ju87B-2.

Above: A Bildberichter at work in the ventral gondola of a He111.

Above right: Kriegsberichter Helmut Grosse doubling as a gunner on board a Junkers Ju88 shot down a Spitfire over England. The Junkers had to ditch in the Channel, however, and Grosse suffered a broken leg. Here he is, hobbling about on crutches.

Right: A Bildberichter sitting beside the pilot of a He111, his Leica camera with telephoto lens at the ready.

Above: After returning from a bombing mission, the task of a Kriegsberichter was not over. He had to write his article recounting his eventful flight, sometimes needing the aid of a crew member for additional details.

Above right: On 25 November 1940 Reichsminister Dr Goebbels received a number of PK-men from the Luftwaffe, the Navy and the Army. Here the Minister of Propaganda is talking to some Sonderführern of the Propaganda-Kompanie.

Right: A Kriegsberichter drawing a Heinkel He111P-2 of KG55. In one of the side-windows the muzzle of an MG15 is visible. This additional armament was mounted on both sides of the fuselage and operated by a fifth crew member.

With the Horst Wessel Geschwader

When World War II broke out, Willi Perchermeier was a professional photographer. As Lt Perchermeier of LwKBK (mot) 4 he was assigned to ZG26, the Horst Wessel Geschwader, in June 1940, but his career as a Kriegsberichter was to be brief. He took photographs of daily activities at ZG26, a number of which are included in this chapter but shortly afterwards he was reassigned to KG76, again not only as a Kriegsberichter but also as gunner.

On 18 August 1940 he took part in a mission with a Ju88, flown by Feldwebel Krebs of 6/KG76, but the aircraft was shot down by Sgt Dymond of No 111 Squadron flying a Hurricane. In 1978 Perchermeier remembered:

Below: Leutnant Willi Perchermeier (to the right) in England in November 1946, back from a POW camp in Canada, to his left is Oblt Isachsen.

Below right: Oberstleutnant Joachim-Friedrich Huth, Kommodore of ZG26. He was a World War I fighter pilot and had only one leg. He was awarded the Ritterkreuz on 11 September 1940.

'On 18 August we had to attack Biggin Hill from a height of 4,000m acting as decoys to attract the British fighters while elsewhere low-level attacks would take place. During the briefing Major Möricke's (Officer commanding II/KG76) last words were "We stick to the slowest aircraft".

'When we arrived over our target Feldwebel Krebs said over the intercom, "Get ready to dive", but he didn't start to dive. I asked "What's happening, why aren't we diving?"

'Krebs said, "Look to the left. Our engine has just been hit". I saw a huge flame behind the engine.

' "Can't you close the fuel cock to stop the fire?"

' "No."

' "What can we do?"

' "We'll drop our bombs while we are flying horizontally," Krebs said, "So that we haven't flown for nothing. We are right over Biggin Hill." Then the bombs were dropped.

' "Can we still get home or do we have to bale out?"

' "No, bale out."

'I waited until the flight engineer had jumped out from below and the wireless operator from behind, then I jettisoned the cab roof.

Above: Morning *Appel* at Maillot airfield, France.

Right: Barrels of fuel were hidden beneath the trees near the airfield.

Below right: While the pilot is already in the cockpit, the gunner boards his Messerschmitt Bf110C-2 with the aid of two members of the groundcrew. The aircraft belongs to III/ZG26.

The pilot had to wait until the co-pilot had jumped, so I said to him, "You'll get out after me, so see you then."

'While hanging below my parachute I scanned the sky but did not see any parachutes nor our machine. Later during the interrogation I was told that immediately after I baled out, a wing fell off the Junkers and the pilot did not succeed in getting out. He was killed. I myself came down with a bang between the shafts of an agricultural cart and, as I wasn't able to roll over and lessen the impact, had to walk with a cane for several weeks.

'Right after coming down I was surrounded by young girls who wanted my flying scarf as a souvenir. Very soon it was torn into numerous little bits so that each of them got something.'

Later Perchermeier was taken to Canada as a POW where he tried unsuccessfully to escape together with Oblt Malischewski. He was released in November 1946.

40

Left: The Horst Wessel Geschwader had a mobile office, installed in a truck.

Below left: A 'Zerstörer' on its way — in this case a Bf110C-2 of I/ZG26.

Below: Servicing Messerschmitt Bf110C-2, W Nr 2146. One wonders if as many willing hands would have been available if the reporter hadn't happened to pass by.

Bottom: Enemy shrapnel has just missed the Bf110's frontal armament of 7.92mm MG17 machine guns.

Above: 'Black men' servicing the
starboard engine of Messerschmitt
Bf110C-2, W Nr 2146.

Above right: The Waffenwart looks
after the Bf110's armament.

Right: After returning from a
mission this Bf110C-4 of II/ZG26
is pushed back beneath some trees;
its fin shows six victories.

Dodging the Balloons

Balloon barrages were a constant danger to low flying Luftwaffe aircraft. Not every pilot was as lucky as Hauptmann Hajo Hermann, Staffelkapitän of 7/KG30, who, in trying to avoid a balloon, actually stalled on top of it but with unbelievable luck was able to gain control of his Ju88 again after falling off the balloon upside down.

What it was like to fly a crippled Dornier Do17 through a balloon barrage is related by another Staffelkapitän after an attack on a power station near London:

'Although I did not want to, shortly before reaching my target I got involved in a dogfight that had started between one of our Zerstörer and some British aircraft. The three British decided to attack me, forgetting the Zerstörer, so a small duel between a Do17, a Bf110 and three English Spitfires began. Suddenly I noticed that my left engine had stopped. In the heat of the fight none of the four of us in the aircraft had seen that a volley from a machine gun had hit the engine . . .

'With one engine out I was quickly forced to lose altitude. We were getting lower and lower and to make matters worse we had to "dance the AA-waltz" just before leaving the city limits. In our condition it should have been easy for the British to put some more shrapnel into our fuselage and elevator, after all everyone knew they were not at all bad shots, but, luckily, they could only manage to do a small amount of damage — enough to lock the elevator as well. The right engine was turning at maximum rpm. But then came something on which nobody had counted — in front of and above us appeared the large sausage shapes of a balloon barrage.

'What now? I'll cut a long story short — you can tell already that we got back safely, but with great difficulty. In the fullest sense of the word, we writhed our way through the labyrinth of balloons and cables. We could not climb above them, the pulling power of the one engine was not strong enough to do that. We had to meander through.

'It was hard work but we did it. When we came through we were only two metres above the ground! The first thing we saw was — far away — the Channel coast. We sweated like bears, that I can assure you. Just imagine — one engine not functioning, the other starting to misfire, the elevator almost stuck and the wind howling through shrapnel holes as large as one's fist.

'Then there was the Channel. Everybody breathed more freely. The wireless operator even reached for his lunch pack. While we were almost crawling on our belly — one could hardly call it flying — the tail gunner suddenly cried out: "Spitfires from behind!" Immediately our machine guns swung towards the attackers. We did not want to sell our hides — or our machine — cheaply. One of

Left: On 28 May 1938 for the first time in 11 years, the Royal Airship Works at Cardington, were opened to the public, in connection with Empire Air Day. Details of the balloon barrage for London's Air Defence — hitherto a closely guarded secret — were revealed to the public. Here visitors look up at the balloons inside the hangars at Cardington.

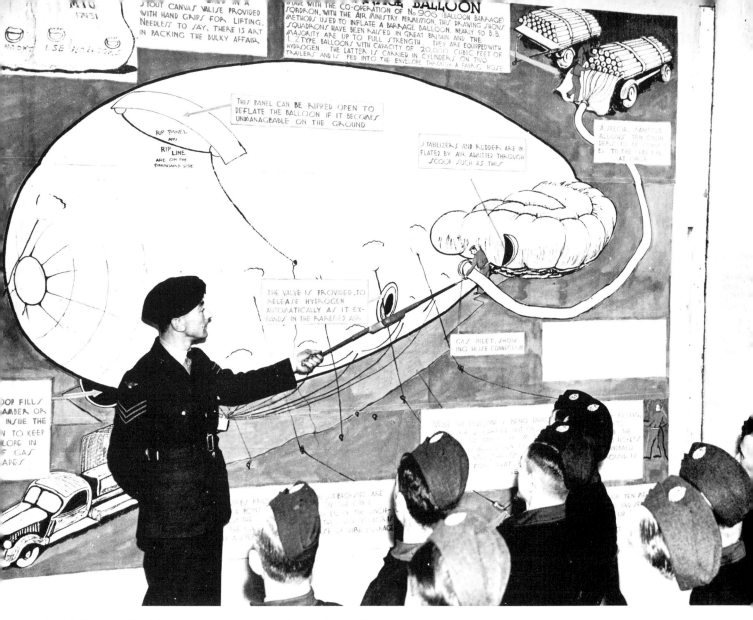

the British pilots dived down on us from a great height and opened fire while he was still far away. We could hardly manoeuvre, only shoot back, shoot back again and hope that we could reach the coast before we hit the deck because our fuel was almost gone.

'The Englishman attacked for the third time. Suddenly he pulled up his machine and curved sharply upwards to disappear into the clouds. We looked at each other in amazement. What was happening? Then two Bf109s appeared, one to the right and one to the left. They passed by us so close that we could see our comrades waving at us from their cockpits. Comradeship between pilots!

'From far away the fighters had seen how we were attacked and how we defended ourselves desperately and they had come to our rescue. Safely covered by the two fighters we reached the coast. But even then a successful emergency landing seemed out of the question. Our good old Do17 was too badly damaged — one undercarriage leg was dangling down and the flaps had also been damaged so badly that it appeared impossible to keep on flying. So then I gave the order, "Bale out".

'The hatch cover flew down, snatched away by the windstream, and one after the other the rear gunner, wireless operator and navigator jumped out. Slowly they soared down to earth under their white parachutes.

'But then, unexpectedly, I found that I could put the machine down and I succeeded in making an emergency landing. I climbed aboard a car that came my way, searched and found my three parachute jumpers and then, finally, was driven home.'

Above left: In July 1939 Sheffield's three balloon barrage squadrons of No 16 Balloon Centre transferred to much larger premises. Photo shows men of the Sheffield Balloon Barrage receiving instruction at their new premises in Bridge Street, Sheffield.

Left: A Messerschmitt Bf109 attacking a balloon. Photograph taken by a Kriegsberichter from the French coast with a telephoto lens.

Above: One of the ground stations for the balloons that ringed London.

Right: At the end of September a storm tore loose many balloons in England and some 60 of them got as far as Sweden. Here is a British balloon that came down near Stockholm.

Overleaf: An LZ balloon over London.

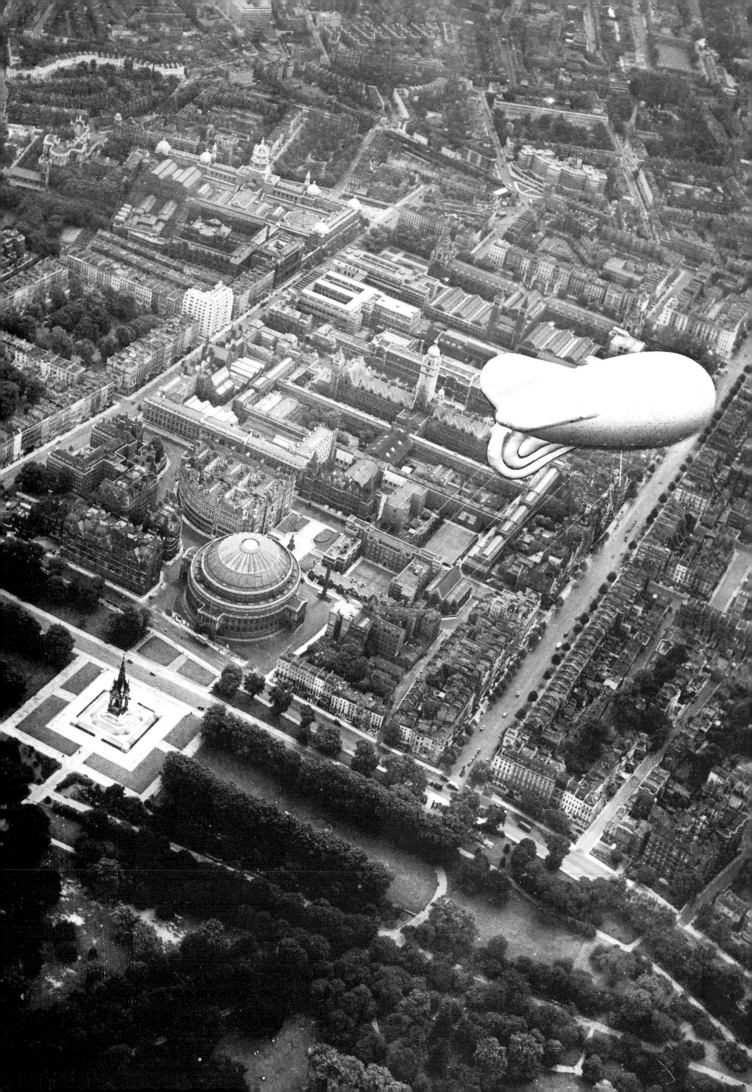

Fighter Cover to Portsmouth

On 12 August, the day before Adlertag was scheduled, an armada of some 100 Junkers Ju88s of KG51, accompanied by about 120 Messerschmitt Bf110s of ZG2 and ZG76 and 25 Bf109s of JG53, attacked England. Some 70 Ju88s bombed Portsmouth after slipping through a gap in the balloon barrage.

Portsmouth had already been attacked on 11 July but this time damage was widespread. Bombs fell on Portsea, Old Portsmouth and parts of Southsea, as well as the Isle of Wight and Gosport. In Portsmouth there were 13 deaths and over 100 people were injured. The ARP Service, well trained and disciplined, did an admirable job.

What it was like to accompany the Junkers in a Bf109 of JG53 is told by Oberleutnant P. von Hofe, some time after the action:
'Our Gruppe was flying cover for the right flank, about 1,500m above the bombers. We were flying with a group of Ju88s that had to carry out a dive-bombing attack.

'Right on time the bomber formation flew over the rendezvous point. The accompanying fighters signalled that the fighter cover had been established. The butterflies in my stomach, felt, I'm sure, by everyone of us, disappeared. They never lasted longer than the first brush with the enemy. We had the impression of quiet peace, but then, suddenly, some black specks appeared amidst the German aircraft and they confirmed that we were now above enemy territory — the enemy AA artillery were sending us their greetings. Tension mounted. Even though the chance of being hit was very small, the little black "Dödels" (things) caused some unrest in the formation.

'There was a haze layer below us which rose to about 3,000m; above it there was a sparkling sky with a 50km visibility. We could see our bombers clearly against the milky haze and some fighters flying lower than us. Faintly visible below was the English landscape — we could see all the obstacles on meadows and fields which had been placed there to hinder a German landing.

'Close together and flying steadily the bomber formation kept on course. No English aircraft had shown up and then, suddenly, somebody reported: "Spitfires behind our dive-bombers." Almost at the same moment we all saw an enemy fighter, recognisable by its outline, closing on the bomber formation from below. At the same time several of our fighters dived down on him. The Spitfire could only fire briefly and then disappeared in a dive.

'Immediately the same thing happened again. The Tommies appeared from below, wanting to damage some of our bombers, force them to leave the formation and finish them off on their own away from the fighters. They did not succeed, as they could manage only short bursts before being driven off. At our altitude everything was quiet, these attacks occurring only near the bomber formation. Suddenly, however, a single aircraft tried to pass below us coming from the right. I saw it was a Hurricane, but I was in an

Right: Hauptmann Bretnütz of II/JG53 in his Bf109E-4. This photo was taken more than two months after the cover mission to Portsmouth. Bretnütz was awarded the Ritterkreuz on 22 October 1940, which he is seen wearing here. He was seriously wounded on 22 June 1941 when attacking a Russian bomber and died five days later after having one leg amputated.

47

unfavourable position so I could fire only a few shots at it as it passed by. The Staffel flying behind us and to the left, dived towards it. The Tommy, however, kept on heading down on the bomber formation. The Staffel had to disengage so as not to be separated from the Gruppe. But at the same time the Hurricane flew straight in front of the guns of the Messerschmitts flying at a lower level. It was shot at by one fighter after the other until it exploded in a ball of fire just above the bomber formation leaving only a large black cloud behind. At the same time around the bomber formation, things were happening — enemy fighters zoomed upwards, fired short bursts at the formation and then disappeared again in the haze. The same thing happened time after time. Every time tracers flew through the sky from the Englishmen's eight guns as well as from the machine guns of the bombers and of the pursuing Messerschmitts.

'In the meantime we had reached our target. This was made clear by AA fire which was growing denser. The formation calmly kept on course. The bombers needed iron nerves to keep going despite the well aimed AA fire, and in order not to let the formation be dispersed. The path followed by our bombers was marked by black clouds of explosions.

' "There is an aerial combat deep below to the left," someone reported. Several aircraft were turning and twisting about: Spitfires and Messerschmitts had come to grips. Three aircraft went down in flames, then the combat was finished. We could not see where the aircraft came to grief, we were too busy ourselves in the middle of a dogfight. It was impossible to say which was the enemy, and which our own side in this short engagement. It was also impossible to take in completely what happened in the next five minutes.

'Six Spitfires dived down from the left, turning towards us. We zoomed up very tightly to the left and they flashed by behind us. We went into a diving turn to the right and the leading Messerschmitts of our Staffel got behind the Spitfires. All our guns were firing. Two Spitfires went down trailing smoke, one of them exploded after a 1,000m dive, the other one flew away leaving white smoke behind it. The other Spitfires turned sharply to meet us and fired away at the rearmost machines of our Staffel. We now got behind the enemy fighters. The Kommandeur set one of them on fire and the English pilot baled out at once. His parachute bloomed under us. The rest of the Tommies dived away and showed us their blue bellies and "peacock's eyes". Two of our aircraft had to report they were leaving the formation as they had been hit badly. The Kommandeur ordered two others to cover them and accompany them home.

'Once again we were flying near the bombers, from which we had been separated by the combat. One of the Ju88s fell back some 200m behind the formation. A long white smoke cloud trailed from the right engine. A hit! Some of our fighters covered the machine.

'The Ju88s curved to the right and then dived down on their target. It was an incredible sight to see the heavy twin-engined bombers dive down steeply, together with the fighters that had to cover them. Huge smoke clouds and dust billows covered the target area — nothing was left standing where those heavy bombs hit. Then the bombers clawed for height back towards the Channel. The one that had been hit before the attack lagged further and further behind; its right propeller was stationary but apparently the machine could maintain its altitude and was still protected by fighters. I hoped it could reach the French coast.

'We searched the sky around us unceasingly. There — some specks were coming towards us. "Several aircraft are turning towards us," someone reported: soon we would have another fight on our hands. Such moments were terribly nerve wracking — but then we saw that they were fighters from another German unit. At a distance English and German fighters looked bloody similar.

Top left: Groundcrew members
starting-up the Daimler-Benz
DB601A engine of a Bf109E-3.
Normal armament was two MG17s
in the fuselage and two MGFF
cannon in the wings. Note the oil
cooler intake scoop.

Centre left: Junkers Ju88s on their
way to Portsmouth seen from a
covering Bf110 of ZG2.

Bottom left: The Portsmouth Air
Raid Protection has already held
realistic exercises in April 1940.

Right: Bombs falling on
Portsmouth harbour.

Below: Luftwaffe bombs falling on
Portsmouth harbour. Such
photographs were often published
at that time in German magazines
like *Signal* and *Der Adler*.

'Then suddenly machines were turning and twisting below the bomber formation. A number of Hurricanes tried to get through our fighter cover and one of them succeeded in shooting down a Ju88 which zoomed earthwards in wild steep turns. We watched it hopefully, waiting to see whether the crew would get out all right. The machine fell and fell, the fall seeming to last an eternity; but at last a parachute appeared — then a second one, but we could not see the place where the machine crashed. Then a Hurricane went down as well. Our fingers itched to get into the fight down below, but we were bound by our mission — unable to leave our stations for fear that the rear cover would then fail, and we would not be in a position to counter surprise attacks by the English. That our Kommandeur's decision was right was proved during the next few seconds: six Hurricanes, coming from immediately behind, passed us going down to attack the fighters below.

'We cut off their path and were suddenly in the middle of a dogfight. Two Hurricanes flew straight ahead; two Messerschmitts were already behind them breathing down their necks. One of the enemy fighters went down, trailing a black smoke cloud, the other one spun away. We could see parts falling off and flying through the air at each twist and turn. In the same moment a report came: "Am hit, have to make an emergency landing," and a Messerschmitt dived down steeply, a white steam cloud streaming behind. For a last time the pilot spoke: "Schweinerei, I have to go down to the Tommies. I give notice of departure to England." Then he baled out to let his aircraft crash on English soil. A parachute glided down.

'Soon afterwards we reached the Channel. The Tommies curved away to land and prepare themselves for the next attack. The small black dots which the coastal AA guns sent upwards did not disturb us any more. Our mission had been accomplished — tension ebbed away.

'We flew over the Channel, the white English coast glistening beneath and the French coast beckoning to us. We were already used to the sight. The blue gleaming breakers greeted us.

'Below, in the middle of the Channel, we saw a spot of yellow. One of our own crews in the water! We went down to see if we could help, but did not need to. This *Seenotfall* (matter for the air-sea rescue) had been observed already by others and reported to the coastal stations. Two *Seenotflugzeuge* (air-sea rescue aircraft) circled above the spot and dropped dinghies. A fighter Staffel covered the action so that the English could not disturb it. From the coast three fast launches were also heading towards the spot. Their long white wakes showed the high speed at which they raced towards their comrades in need of help.

'We hedge-hopped across the coast and soon after landed at our forward landing strip *(Feldflugplatz)*. During the debriefing by the Kommandeur and the Staffelkapitäne the things that had happened during the past hours came back again vividly. The pilots had a short rest and then a new mission order came through. We had to fly against England again.'

That day, JG53 lost two Bf109s, one of them being flown by Hauptmann Harder, Gruppenkommandeur of III/JG53, who was killed. KG51 even lost its Geschwader Kommodore, Oberst Dr Fisser, on the same day when his Ju88 was shot down by a Hurricane of No 213 Squadron.

During the attack on Portsmouth, Junkers Ju88A-1, 9K+BS (WNr4078) of III/KG51 flown by Lt Seidel, was shot down by AA fire, the four crew members dying. Three months before on 10 May 1940, Lt Seidel had made a historic mistake. That day 20 He111s of III/KG51 had taken-off from Landsberg and Bad Wörishofen to bomb the French airfield of Dijon-Longvic, the alternative target being the airfield of Dôle-Tavaux. Attacks by French fighters, thunderstorms over the black forest and the tiredness of the crews were the reasons why a Kette of three He111s led by Lt Seidel lost its bearings and bombed the airfield of Freiburg in Germany, thinking they bombed Dijon-Longvic. 22 children, 13 women and 22 men were killed by the bombs. Before the day had passed the OKW stated :

'On 10 May, three enemy aircraft attacked the open city of Freiburg im Breisgau ... The German Luftwaffe will avenge this act in the same way ...'

The German propaganda machine was quick to lay the responsibility of Lt Seidel's mistake upon the other side! Lt Seidel's error was another step in the escalation of the bombing war.

The raid upon Portsmouth however was commented upon by *Der Adler* in its 3 September 1940 issue, showing aerial photographs taken during the actual attack.

Below: Members of the staff of KG51 discussing the Portsmouth raid after returning to Orly airfield. In the background can be seen one of the airship sheds.

Attacking RAF Driffield

Without doubt 15 August 1940 saw the most bitter fighting of the Battle of Britain. The main Luftwaffe bomber targets were still Fighter Command airfields but due to poor German intelligence some airfields where no fighters were stationed at that time were also attacked, one example being RAF Driffield, a Bomber Command airfield in Yorkshire. The attack was carried out by 50 Ju88s of KG30 stationed at Aalborg in occupied Denmark. The mission is recounted by Oberleutnant Rudolf Kratz of Stab/KG30:

'The weather was dreadful — so bad that one wouldn't dream of putting a dog out in it. It rained, it poured down. Dirty grey rivulets ran through the soil. Under the wing of a bomber a sentry sought refuge from the rain and from this vantage point he saw human shapes running towards him from the hangars. He recognised them as members of the "black band", the groundcrews — *Bordmonteure* and *Erste Warte* (flight engineers and groundcrew chiefs) who had been ordered to the aircraft at daybreak.

' "What are you doing over here in this appalling weather?" he shouted to them.

' "Looking for Easter-eggs, a morose voice answered sarcastically, but another said "Mensch, don't ask so many questions, we have to get the kites ready."

'Almost freezing, the sentry walked away and watched his comrades remove the covering tarpaulins with their wet fingers and, soaking wet, loosen the tie-down ropes. But their curses had a

serious ring, music to accompany their toils. Every man knew the value of fast and accurate work and how important it was.

'Against all expectations the rain stopped falling. Some engines were running already when the crews arrived at their aircraft in their cumbersome flying overalls and boots for a mission against the enemy. They all knew their target but what would the next hours bring them? The speed of events did not allow any serious thoughts on the subject.

' "Mind your fingers!" cried the crew chief and slammed the entry hatch of the ventral gondola shut. This act enclosed the men in the bomber and shut them off from the outside world — but they didn't have time to think about it. Each of them had to prepare for the flight. The pilot's call *"Alles klar"* (everything ready) pulled them together and from each battle position came through the awaited call: *"Alles Klar"*.

Below: A Hanomag SS100 tractor is used to drag an SC500 bomb across the grass airfield to a waiting Junkers Ju88A-1. Two bombs are already in place on the external bomb racks under the port wing. An additional 7.92mm MG15 machine gun can be seen in the cockpit roof.

Left: Writing 'dedications' on bombs has been a time-honoured tradition since World War I. Here groundcrew members of KG54 'Totenkopf' are chalking their 'best wishes' on some SC250 bombs in front of a Junkers Ju88. They read 'Greetings from the Totenkopf Geschwader', 'In order that we should live, you dogs have to die', and 'One has to give presents to those one loves'.

Below: A Junkers Ju88 crew member, already in full flying gear, is helping a Feldwebel with his flying suit.

' "I would not like to be in England tonight," the wireless operator said through the intercom as he watched the large number of bombers rolling towards the take-off area, with revving engines.

'Now our aircraft was ready to take-off. Exactly on time the engines roared away and drew us and our load of bombs into the sky, leaving the airfield behind us. One by one the rest of the aircraft took-off until behind us a string of aircraft followed at regular intervals. Slowly they got closer together and soon the formation had been established. The changing landscape was worth looking at, but not now, perhaps on the way back. We did not have the time for that at this point in the mission; our thoughts were set on course, altitude, weather and the like. The machine guns were readied for action. A few shots into the water? The coast had already left behind — and yes, it still shot all right, why shouldn't it?

' "*FT klar*" (wireless transmitter all right) reported the wireless operator and things were cosy on board the aircraft. There wasn't any drama — no stick or machine gun "convulsively gripped" and no "sharp profiles of energetic men" as the correspondents would lead one to believe. The many missions we had flown together, the many battles fought together made talking unnecessary. We understood each other, through a simple gesture, through a smile.

'The land had disappeared some time ago and the white caps of breaking waves also vanished. Seen from above the sea had a strange sense of immobility. The intense cold, a sign of high altitude, made us think about oxygen.

' "All right, masks on." Unfortunately with masks donned one could no longer whistle or play tunes on the mouth-organ, but we made do with a murmured song. Time went by slowly.

' "How long till the English coast?"

' "Twenty minutes."

The ammunition drums for the machine guns were placed within reach. Everyone was more attentive now. English fighters might appear from anywhere.

'Visibility had become poor. The water and the sky merged into each other without a trace of horizon. It was misty. Any moment now the English coast would appear below.

'Had our navigation been correct? Nothing to be seen yet. Aircraft upon aircraft were flying with us. They wobbled up and down, carrying death. Our target: an English airfield.

'What would it look like? We knew its layout accurately from the aerial photos taken during reconnaissance flights — every hangar, every barracks. But was it a sundrenched field, with aircraft standing in front of the hangars, groundcrews busy as ever? Did they know we were on our way? Maybe the fighters had already taken-off, and shells were already being loaded into the barrels of the AA guns?

' "The coast. The initial point." No time left for thinking — there lay England, the lion's den. But the eagles were going to attack the lion in his lair and wound him grievously.

"Fighters to starboard…" Three specks overflew us, disappeared to the rear and, after a diving turn, hung behind us.

' "Your turn now". The words disappeared in the rattle of our machine guns. In short bursts the volleys flew towards the first fighter. He turned away and the second one took his place. This one's fire was ineffective as well and both passed below and were shot at by our ventral gunner. Like hornets they swooshed through our formation, the roundels on their fuselage looking like eyes.

' "Five fighters to port above," reported the wireless operator calmly.

' "Dammit," the pilot said, but did not get agitated. We kept on flying towards our target. Staring before us we tried to locate the airfield amidst the ragged clouds.

' "There, the field, below us."

'The target at last — the fighters were beginning to be a real nuisance. The time had come now. I did not give one single Pfennig for the life of those below — drop the bombs, away with the blessing! The aircraft went into a dive, speed rapidly building up, and the wind roared and howled around us. The hangars grew and grew. They were still standing. The AA guns were firing away at us, but they were too late.

'A jolt — the bombs were free, the steel bodies whistling down. Below all hell was let loose. Like an inferno, steel hit steel, and stones. Bomb upon bomb exploded, destroying and tearing apart what they hit. Hangar walls and roofs crumpled like tin sheets, pieces flying through the air. Aircraft were shattered by a hail of splinters. Barracks tumbled down, enormous smoke and dust clouds rose like mushrooms. Here and there explosions and flames shot up. The airfield and the hangars were already badly hit but bombs kept falling from the bombers that followed us, kept raining

down in a horrible shower. Fire from exploding ammunition burst upwards like torches. The English AA artillery had been eliminated, their firing positions turned into craters.

'The sun shone into our cabin. The enemy fighters had been got rid off. Below us lay the wide sea. How beautiful the Earth can be. Hands loosened their grip on the machine guns. What happened just a few minutes ago lay behind us and we relaxed. The engines were running evenly, we were flying home. The airfield didn't exist any more; that was the result. The camera held proof thereof.

'The seemingly endless expanse of water and the regular beat of the engines heightened the impression of unworldliness. Earthly worries seemed far away and ridiculously small. A kind of soothing weariness left room only for the most simple thoughts but could not drive away the steady attentiveness. Minutes crawled by. The nearer we came to our base, the more we felt the need to express our impressions. A burning question was the one about our comrades, their aircraft, their results...

'The last technical achievement of the flight mattered little — back home the weather was good and we could trust our aircraft to get us back safely.'

Oberleutnant Kratz who wrote the above report had joined the Reichswehr in 1934 and had transferred to the Luftwaffe the following year. In 1937 he had been trained in blind-flying, while on Lufthansa routes, as did so many Luftwaffe pilots at that time. It was a perfect camouflage. 39 years after writing the report, he had become a dentist in Bad Salzuflen and he remembered:
'I wrote the report for my own entertainment, but it got in front of Oblt Loebel who gave it to a Kriegsberichter. From there it found its way into the Jahrbuch of the Luftwaffe. Today I find it too emphatic and bombastic. But then those times were filled with heroism, the call of duty and big words.'

About the actual attack on RAF Driffield he remembers amongst other things: 'The so-called *Bienenschwarmtechnik* had been ordered. The rearmost machines continually placed themselves below those flying in front, who fell back in their turn. In this way the formation was continuously in motion and this should have made attacks by RAF fighters more difficult.'

Of the 50 Ju88s that had taken-off from Aalborg, seven were shot down over England while three others were severely damaged and had to crash land in the Netherlands, near Oldenburg and at Aalborg. As a result of these severe losses, KG30 was withdrawn to be redeployed in Holland (Gilze-Rijen and Eindhoven) during September.

On that 15 August, Hauptmann Restemayer, Gruppenkommandeur of I/ZG76 was killed when his Messerschmitt Bf110D crashed into the sea off the Durham coast, shot down by Spitfires of No 72 Squadron. He had gained fame when, together with Oberleutnant Schleif and Oberleutnant Trautloft, he had won first place in the International Alpine Ralley for the formation flying of military aircraft at the Zürich/Dübendorf flying meet in 1937. The three of them were flying the then sensational Bf109.

Right: Also on this day Hauptmann W. Restemeyer, Gruppenkommandeur of I/ZG76 was killed when his Bf110D was shot down by Spitfires of No 72 Squadron and crashed into the sea off Durham. Oblt Schleif was killed in action on the first day of the Polish campaign and only Oblt H. Trautloft survived the war. Photo shows Restemeyer (middle) with Oblt Schleif (left) and Oblt Trautloft (right) after the team won the International Alpine Ralley for military formations, in July 1937 at Dübendorf. *Photopress Zürich*

Above: Major Dönch reports to Göring when the latter visited KG30 at Oldenburg airfield. On Dönch's left and Göring's right can be seen in the background Oberleutnant Rudolf Kratz, who wrote the report. *Dr Rudolf Kratz*

Stukas Against Radar Stations

Amongst other targets, Junkers Ju87Bs of StG2 attacked the CH radar at Ventnor on 16 August 1940. Five Stukas dropped some 22 bombs damaging the station so that it was unserviceable for seven days. An interception by Spitfires of No 152 Squadron was warded off by escorting Bf109s of JG53. The following account of the attack was written by PK-Mann Curt Strohmeyer:

'Once again we had been detailed to destroy a wireless station on the south coast of the British Isles. The approach had to be made at a height of 4,000m. After the attack we had to fly back at low level. Wind speeds and directions, very important elements when dropping bombs, were given and then every crew sped towards their aircraft.

'Minutes later the earth glided past below us as if in a dream. Freed from gravity we soared through the heavens above the coastline and above the endless sea. Then we were over the target — large antennae masts and nearby transmitting stations.

'When the Kommandeur was right above the target he put his aircraft into a dive and slowly the machine nosed down. All the other aircraft of the unit followed close behind him. I watched the Kommandeur's bombs disappearing in the middle of a large building — probably the machinery room and seconds later an immense smoke cloud erupted from it. Then our bombs were falling away. After flattening out I could still see, for a moment, the cruel and yet beautiful sight. Nothing was to be seen of the wireless station. Where only minutes ago it had stood, only dense smoke was to be seen. I saw the last bomb crashing down right beside a wireless mast. The mast was lifted bodily and then fell into the smoke cloud above what was once a wireless station.

'We hugged the ground on our way back to the Channel. There — English Spitfires and Hurricanes! The German fighters covering us attacked at once and a wild dogfight developed. Spitfires swooped through our formation followed by our Bf109s. Here and

Below: Their cameras equipped with powerful telescopic lenses, the German Kriegsberichter were able to take photos of the English radar stations from the French side of the Channel.

there a Spitfire escaped from its pursuer and I watched two of them attacking a Ju87 which was flying behind me. One of the two machines was turned away by the well-aimed fire of the wireless operator, but at the same moment the other Spitfire reached an excellent shooting position and fired a volley into the Stuka's fuel tanks. The Stuka burnt fiercely and shortly afterwards crashed into the sea. The crew, however, was able to bale out. But the Englishman wasn't able to enjoy his success for long, for at the same moment as the Stuka disappeared into the waves, a Bf109 was on the Spitfire's tail and despite violent attempts to escape from his enemy by weaving, the German fighter put him into the Channel half a minute later. Just then I got a Spitfire in my gunsights. After a few bursts I saw that I'd hit him. A long thin smoke trail followed his aircraft, but I lost sight of him in the general mêlée.

'The English coast disappeared behind us and the enemy fighters, which only minutes ago were on our tails, did not seem to be particularly aggressive. They turned away and soon vanished over the horizon. Slowly the enormous tension ebbed away and only now could we feel happy about the successful attack on the wireless station. The fight against the English had only lasted minutes — 10, maybe 14 of them had been shot down. All but one of our "Jolanthes" (Junkers Ju87) returned. The fighters zoomed past waggling their wings. We waved back. The fight had lasted only minutes but once again it had been a memorable meeting with our unknown bold comrades of the Fighter Arm.'

Above: The pilot of a Junkers Ju87B-1 at the controls of his aircraft. *Bundesarchiv*

Left: Members of the groundcrew topping up the engine oil-tank of a Junkers Ju87B-1.

Above right: Groundcrew loading up a Junkers Ju87B-1 with SC50 bombs on the ETC50 bomb rack.

Right: Adjusting the wing-mounted, electro-pneumatic-operated Rheinmetall-Borsig 7.92mm MG17 machine guns of a Junkers Ju87B-1 W Nr 439.

Top right: Junkers Ju87B-2s on their way to their target. The Stukas had been particularly successful during the campaigns in continental Europe but proved very vulnerable when attacking targets in England.

Centre right: Junkers Ju87B-1 pushed back in its dispersal area after returning from a mission. Note the size of the aircraft in comparison with the groundcrew members, a big aircraft indeed.

Below: Chief of Staff to Generalmajor Dipl-Ing Wolfram von Richthofen, commander of VIII Fliegerkorps which grouped most of the Junkers Ju87 units, was Oberstleutnant Hans Seidemann. As a Reichswehroffizier, Seidemann had started participating in sports flying events in 1925, flying a Udet U-12 Flamingo. Later he graduated to the Messerschmitt Bf108, the Ago Ao192 and, in July 1937 at Dübendorf, even to the Bf109. On 1 November 1938 he became von Richthofen's Chief of Staff in the Condor Legion. Seidemann was no stranger to England. Flying Bf108 D-IOSA, he had won the London-Isle of Man Race on 29 May 1937. Participating in the same event on 4 June 1938 he came seventh while flying the Ago Ao192V2 D-OCTB. This photograph shows Seidemann being welcomed by friends at the Berlin Tempelhof airport when he returned after winning the Isle of Man Race in 1937.

A Staffelkapitän over England

In July 1940, 3/JG2 got a new Staffelkapitän, Oberleutnant Helmut Wick. He had obtained his first victory on 22 November 1939 and his 13th on 13 June 1940, all on the Western Front. He had already shot down a Spitfire over England on 17 July, although at that time he was not supposed to be flying there. His first big sweep over that country came on 18 August 1940. Wick described the action as follows:

'18 August dawned and a large scale attack against England — at last the damned patrols along the coast were over. Early in the morning Staffel after Staffel took-off, Gruppe after Gruppe, Geschwader after Geschwader. Bombers, Zerstörer, fighters. Wherever we looked, the sky was filled with aircraft. The German Luftwaffe was on a large scale attack against the English.

'On the outward-bound flight I did not think to ask myself if all these machines were German but, shortly before arriving at the English coast, I saw a green spot down on the surface of the water and was somewhat startled. Down there a poor devil who had been shot down was swimming about and trying to attract attention with his dye packet. I looked around and — devil take it — like a shower of rain 12 Spitfires dived down on us.

'Immediately I turned into them. When I finished the turn I saw a Spitfire hanging behind a Bf109 and higher up the same thing, a Spitfire behind a Messerschmitt. Almost at the same time both German fighters did the only thing possible. Suddenly they were gone. The two Spitfires disappeared. The others had dived down past us. This was more or less the beginning — what followed happened much faster than I can tell it. All over, wherever one looked, there was an unbelievable twisting and turning of aircraft over aircraft, our own and the enemy's but the enemy were in the majority. The English fighter force was still completely intact and could muster a significantly superior force at specific points. We were now confronted with just such a force.

'Three Englishmen flew towards me, very close together. I pulled the stick full backwards and positioned myself behind them. A fast look to the right and to the left — for the next few seconds the sky was clear. I dived faster, got the leader in my gunsight, depressed the buttons — he plunged down, and the two others accompanying him were gone. I zoomed upwards. Something was going on to the right. I could hardly believe my eyes. The sky was filled with Spitfires and amongst them a few poor Messerschmitts. Into the gaggle to get the chaps out! Immediately a Spitfire was sitting behind me. I got away, with full throttle — in front of me another Spitfire and behind? Dammit. Another was sitting on my tail again so I dived and I made a climbing turn. To the right, just beside my cockpit, strange white lines appeared. More and more — but they stayed to the right hand side. I looked behind me quickly. Another Spitfire was sitting there and spraying his tracers around my ears, tracers which we call corpse-fingers (Leichenfinger). I looked left. Holy terror! Behind me to the left hung three Spitfires. I was

Left: Hauptmann Helmut Wick holding his walking stick which had a notch for each of his victories. Wick is wearing the Ritterkreuz which he was awarded on 27 August 1940.

surrounded and in a bad spot. Throttle fully open I made a sharp left turn and the tracers flashed past above me. I would certainly thank the gods if my mother's son got away from this mess unhurt.

'The climb had given me some room to manoeuvre but still my few comrades were fighting against a more numerous enemy. Whenever I tried to interfere I got Spitfires on my tail and had to get away. Then a Bf109 flashed by at an incredible rate and behind it a Spitfire. It was sent by heaven — I got behind the Tommy, got him in my gunsight and after a few volleys he nosed down.

'We had more room now, so I could follow the Englishman with my eyes. He splashed down in the water and even from my altitude I could see the white foam. Then no more — nothing betrayed the fact that a gallant pilot had died a heroic death at that spot.

'Time to fly home. But how to get my flock together? The formation had dispersed totally, everywhere aircraft twisted and turned. I used my wireless set "Dismiss. Back to base." My clock showed that it was time to fly back. In the middle of the Channel I saw a gaggle of aircraft flying parallel to the coast, evidently fighters. Surely they couldn't be Messerschmitts? I glanced at the fuel indicator. I could risk paying them a visit. A sharp turn placed me behind the rearmost threesome. Then I got close — dammit — it wasn't the rearmost! More of them were following behind. So I dived and zoomed up behind them. This time they really were the end section. I got the leader in my sights and fired. Apparently I hit the pilot because the aircraft dived uncontrollably and crashed into the water. But now I had the whole unit behind me and again I saw tracers flashing by, but my aircraft's superior speed took me away from further attacks. The Tommies gave up and flew home as well.

Top left: Hauptmann Wick using both hands to describe a dogfight.

Bottom left: Major Helmut Wick posing for the photographers after he had been awarded the Eichenlaub on 6 October and after he had been appointed Geschwaderkommodore of JG2 'Richthofen'.

Below centre: Major Helmut Wick listening to Generalfeldmarschall Hugo Sperrle, commander of Luftflotte 3.

Right: A pilot who also lost his life while flying over the North Sea, like Helmut Wick, was Leutnant Franz von Werra of II/JG2. He is seen here with 'Simba', a young lion cub used as a mascot. On 5 September 1940 he was made POW after having been forced to land near Marsden. Later on he managed to escape from Canada and returned to Germany after an eventful journey. On 25 October 1941, while flying over the North Sea, the engine of his Bf109 failed and he went down to a watery grave near Vlissingen.

Below: This factory-fresh Bf109E-4 of I/JG3, surrounded by bovine visitors on an airfield in France, has had its *Stammkennzeichen* (basic registration) painted over to be replaced by the special markings for *Jagdverbände* (fighter units). These *Stammkennzeichen* are often erroneously designated 'radio call signs' or 'factory codes'.

'This was my 13th aerial combat and my 17th victory. I have to confess that after this dogfight I was happy to be able to get back to base, as I was exhausted. When I touched down, it seemed that I was becoming a famous man, because the moment I landed the interviews started. From the Kriegsberichterkompanie of the Luftflotte came photographers, reporters and radio-men. This was something new to me. I had never stood in the limelight and had no intention of doing so, it didn't suit me. But the friendly reporters and some hints from upstairs made it clear to me that it was necessary. And I realised that people at home had the right to hear about our combat. After all, it was only natural that the Kriegsberichter were interested in those pilots who had the highest number of victories to their credit. But this insight did not change the fact that my first talk into the microphone seemed harder to me than obtaining an aerial victory. But then, when the tape was played off, I rather liked it.

'It was also around this time that my *Katschmarek* (wingman) who had accompanied me on all combats from the beginning began to insult me. After my first victories my Staffel had presented me with a thick walking cane, which got the honorific title of *Schwarmstock*. After every victory a V was carved into the wood together with the date, type and the airfield from which I had started. Leutnant Fiby, who had taken the carving upon himself began saying that he couldn't get anything more on the "Stock". I should shoot down either Hurricanes alone or Spitfires alone, not both. If I stuck to one type he could get more on the stick as he could use dittos. Once he came to me with a worried look on his

face and said to me: "You know, it is great that you shoot down the British so often, but I'm running into trouble now because the stock will soon be too short." '

The meteoric rise of the Luftwaffe's first fighter ace, Helmut Wick, can be followed through the despatches of the OKW.

26 August 1940
'The Jagdgeschwader Richthofen achieved its 250th victory during yesterday's aerial combats. Oberleutnant Wick obtained his 19th and 20th kills.

6 October 1940
'Hauptmann Wick shot down five fighters in aerial combat in one day thus getting his 41st kill.'

8 November 1940
Major Wick on 6 and 7 November obtained his 48th-53rd victories by shooting down six enemy aircraft.

16 November 1940
'The Jagdgeschwader Freiherr von Richthofen obtained its 500th victory under the leadership of Major Wick.'

4th December 1940
'The Kommodore of Jagdgeschwader Richthofen, Major Wick, did not return from a flight into enemy territory after his 56th victory. The German Luftwaffe has lost one of its most daring and successful fighter pilots. Major Wick, who has been decorated with the *Eichenlaub zum Ritterkreuz des Eisernen Kreuzes* for his heroism in the fight for the future of the German people, will live on as an example to the German people and especially to German youth.'

Below: Engine maintenance performed on a Bf109E.

Below right: This leutnant is being helped to don his parachute before climbing into his Bf109E-3.

Low~Level Attack

Sunday, 18 August, saw a daring low-level attack by the Luftwaffe. There were often some Kriegsberichter on board the bombers that attacked from extremely low altitudes and in cinemas all over Germany and occupied Europe, striking UFA newsreels were shown, for example the one for the first week of November 1940.

This low-level attack was flown by nine Dornier Do17s of 9/KG76 against RAF Kenley. Several of the Dorniers operating against Henley carried a Kriegsberichter on board. This is what one of them wrote about the attack:

'The mission flown by the Ninth Staffel of our Kampfgeschwader will forever remain a shining example of the German airmen's spirit. All alone, without being covered by German fighters, the nine Dorniers swept over England, at only a few metres height, for the first daring low-level raid against England...

'England was so near that we could almost touch it. Sometimes hardly two metres below the wings of our heavily loaded aircraft. After we had jumped the steep coast from sea level, we were able to study in detail England's coastal defences. We roared so low across the south of England, hopping over rows of trees and every hedge, that one of the crews brought back amongst the splintered glass of the glazed nose, some leaves from an English tree whose top the machine had touched on his wild flight.

'It was a destructive attack on an airfield near London. Seven hangars and the barracks were blown to pieces and the field was

Below: Flying low above the waves, Dornier Do17Z-2s of 9/KG76, are approaching the English coast near Beachy Head.

Right: Only minutes later the Dorniers were streaking over the English countryside heading for RAF Kenley. This photograph is of Southease & Rodmell station on the Southern Railway on the former London Brighton & South Coast Railway beween Newhaven and Lewes.

Below: This much publicised photo shows bombs exploding in the dispersal area of RAF Kenley, a sector airfield. The photograph has, however, been retouched and the nearest two large smoke clouds have been added to the original negative. *Bundesarchiv*

Bottom: An impression by a Kriegsberichter draughtsman of the low-level attack.

covered with bomb craters. All hell was let loose on the airfield. The bombs dropped by the first Kette left no two bricks of the hangars and the control tower standing together. The second Kette that followed at a short distance saw how scores of totally surprised and bewildered Englishmen rushed out of their living quarters into the air-raid trenches. Inexorably bombs fell among this seething mass of people. Wooden parts of the barrack units, steel helmets, uniforms, human bodies — all whirled through the air. We of the third Kette, roaring through the smoke and dust of the explosions, saw these visions in fractions of seconds and were able to save part of our bomb load for targets on the way home.

'And then we stormed right into the middle of a numerically superior unit of English fighters which were in the process of taking-off. Our closely flying Ketten dispersed. Each separate crew now had four or even more Spitfires or Hurricanes against it. Fast as lightning the bewildering multi-coloured network of tracer trails flashed to and fro, only a few metres above English soil, above the sprawling suburbs of London, above villages and towns.

'Time and time again the English dived upon homeward flying aircraft. Every time bursts of fire from our rear machine guns received them. Like a hailstorm beating against a window pane, the machine gun bullets of the enemy fighters' eight guns hammered into the wings of our machines. Many of our men stayed at their machine gun posts despite injuries — firing away with their left hands when their right had been hit . . .

'We lost our pursuers before reaching the coast and then the water of the Channel was below us. But even the flight home saw heroic deeds — one wounded pilot brought back his badly shot-up machine with one engine faltering and despite incapacitating wounds. Above the sea of houses of London, one observer, Feldwebel Illg, took over the controls of the aircraft from its mortally wounded pilot. He was sitting in the pilot's seat for the first time in his life, but mastered that seemingly impossible task and saved his comrades and the machine. Nearly every aircraft showed the marks of numerous hits and the Staffel had to pay for this attack with the death of its Staffelkapitän, Oblt Lamberty.'

Indeed, 9/KG76 paid heavily for this raid. Hurricanes of Nos 32 and 61 Squadrons shot down two Dorniers, including the one flown by Staffelkapitän Oberleutnant Lamberty, and two went into the

Right: While the low-level attack against the RAF sector airfield at Kenley was taking place, attacks at high level were being carried out against Malling, Croydon and Biggin Hill. This photo shows bombs falling towards Biggin Hill.

Below: One of the surviving Dornier Do17Z-2s speeding towards the Channel is flying much lower than the cliff tops of the Seven Sisters cliffs.

Bottom: Photograph taken during another raid at low level, only a short distance from the entrance to the Great Yarmouth harbour.

Channel. Of the remaining four, three made crash-landings in France and it was only the Dornier flown flown by Feldwebel Illg that made a more or less normal arrival.

It is an amazing fact that on board the crippled Dornier flown home to its base at Cormeilles-en-Vexin by Feldwebel Illg, a Kriegsberichter was flying as the machine gunner. He wrote this about his experience:

'When I saw London for the first time, it was lying hardly 100m below the broad wings of our bomber. The warm August sun had burnt away all the clouds from the sky. Through the light mist, the roofs of the metropolis glimmered upwards. We flew across the grey mass of houses of the eastern suburbs to where the bewildering network of hundreds upon hundreds of streets lost itself in the poisonous green surface of the Plumstead Marshes on the south bank of the River Thames. From a height of 100m the sight of the most imposing entanglement of houses in Europe should have been overwhelming — but at that time we had other things to worry about.

'A few minutes before a machine gun bullet had ripped open the arm and chest of our pilot and it was the feet of a dying man buckled to the rudder pedals that steered our course. London glided past below us while we were busy getting the pilot from his seat. We fired round after round at the attacking English fighters. Only occasionally could we see anything of the city through the wide open floor of the bomber from which the flight engineer had already jettisoned the hatch to prepare for the parachute jump that might become necessary.

'All this was very exciting but most important to us at the time was the urgent necessity to replace the dead pilot with a crew member who could fly the machine and bring us home.

'We took little part in what was happening in the air or on the ground. It was 18 August and not a single bomb had yet been dropped on the docks and warehouses along the River Thames.'

When the pilot collapsed on the steering wheel, Oberfeldwebel Wilhelm-Friedrich Illg had, as quick as lightning, gripped the wheel and standing upright, had forced the bomber, which at that time was flying some 10m off the ground, upwards, at the same time jettisoning the eight bombs still on board. By avoiding the balloon barrage he got over the suburbs of London.

Oblt Magin, the pilot, died after the landing on his way to hospital. Oberfeldwebel Illg was promoted Leutnant and awarded the Ritterkreuz for his singular action. His exploit was made into an episode of the German film *Kampfgeschwader Lützow* which showed the tribulations of an imaginary Luftwaffe bomber Geschwader. The film was made by Hans Bertram who had been an advisor to the Chinese Naval Aviation from 1927 to 1933 and had made an unsuccessful attempt to fly a float-equipped Junkers F13 to China in 1931, an attempt that ended in a crash in a monsoon storm in the harbour of Vizagapatnam. The following year he had attempted to fly from Germany to Australia and had been lost on the uninhabited north coast of Australia where he had to fight hunger, thirst, illness and crocodiles for 53 days before being rescued. He wrote a book about his adventures and no less than 900,000 copies were sold in air-conscious Germany.

His film *Kampfgeschwader Lützow* was a propaganda film premiered in Berlin on 28 February 1941. Not present at the premiere was Leutnant Illg. A week after his exploit he had been made a prisoner of war after being shot down near London, leaving him little time to enjoy his Ritterkreuz.

Above: Many Kriegsberichter accompanied the Luftwaffe bomber crews on their raids over England and provided many German and other European cinema-goers with excellent film footage, sometimes taken at the risk of the Kriegsberichter's life. This is a still picture from the UFA-Wochenschau (UFA Weekly Newsreel) for the first week of October 1940.

Centre left: Scene from the film *Kampfgeschwader Lützow* showing a burning Polish P-37-Los bomber.

Bottom left: Oberleutnant Hans-Siegfried Ahrends, the pilot of the Do17 that led the right vic of three. His aircraft suffered a direct AA hit and shortly after was struck by a parachute and cable device. All aboard were killed when the aircraft crashed at the boundary of Kenley airfield.

Left: Leutnant Friedrich-Wilhelm Illg who took over from the dying pilot while the Do17 was flying low over London's suburbs.

Defiants Again

In the course of August 1940, shortly before his 28th birthday, Hauptmann Günther Lützow — Franzl to his friends — was appointed Kommodore of JG3 based on airstrips in the Pas-de-Calais. One of the first times he led his Geschwader into battle was on 24 August when Defiants were encountered. This is how he described the action:

'The Staffelkapitäne gathered at the Gefechtsstand. The Kommandeur gave the orders. We were to act as escort for a bomber unit that had to attack military objectives in and near London. Nothing really new, our daily bread. Therefore nothing much had to be said, as the Staffelkapitäne didn't have much to ask. I was going to be flying with the *Führungsschwarm* (the leading foursome). Right on time the first machine started to take-off, its tail came up and it lifted off. One after the other, the unit followed suit. Flying in a wide arc the Gruppe assembled over the airfield. By wireless I ascertained that the two other Gruppen of the Geschwader were following. Below us to the left the bomber unit appeared. It set course towards London. I looked behind. The Gruppen had taken up their ordered stations. Everywhere threesomes and foursomes of Messerschmitts were swarming around the "big brothers". Now the English could come at us if they wanted!

'The sky was radiantly blue. Deep below us hung a few scattered clouds, and we could make out clearly the abrupt coastline at Dover. Then the Thames estuary loomed up to the right and the first reports reached me: "Spitfires above us." At this moment I couldn't place them and flew to the other side of the bomber formation. From there I could see that there was already some fighting going on to the left and below. The first English formations

Below left: The Geschwaderkommodore of Jagdgeschwader 3, Hauptmann Günther Lützow, chatting with some fellow-officers. Jagdgeschwader 3 is often referred to as Jagdgeschwader Udet. It got this name only after Udet's suicide on 17 November 1941, a year after the Battle of Britain.

Below: The chalky coasts of France and England provided an impressive background for this Kette of Bf109Es.

Above: On the day of Lützow's account, 24 August 1940, Oblt Wilhelm Balthasar, Gruppenkommandeur of III/JG3, obtained his 24th victory. As a Condor Legion pilot he had shot down four Martin bombers in one day near Teruel on 7 February 1938. Early in 1939 he made a series of flights around and over Africa in a Siebel Fh104. This photograph shows the Siebel and its crew on their return to Tempelhof on 7 March 1939. From left to right: Oberleutnant Balthasar, Feldwebel Anhäuser and Oberleutnant Kaldrack. Wilhelm Balthasar lost his life on 3 July 1941 when his Bf109F folded up during an aerial combat over France. During the Battle of Britain Hauptmann Rolf Kaldrack was Gruppenkommandeur of III/ZG76. He was killed on 3 February 1942 near Toropez, Russia, when the MiG-1 he had just shot down rammed his Bf110.

Right: The Normandy orchards provided excellent cover for these Messerschmitt Bf109s of JG3. When necessary netting was draped over the trees for additional camouflage. Nearest aircraft is a Bf109E-4 and the one in the background a Bf109E-1.
Bundesarchiv

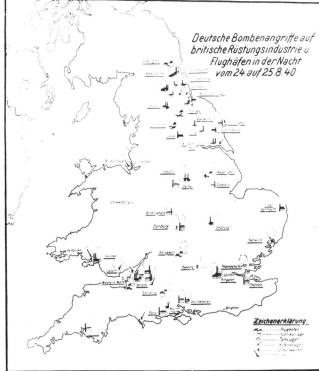

Above: One who almost needed the services of the air/sea rescue was Oberleutnant Eduard Neumann, Gruppenkommandeur of II/JG27, when a round of his 2cm MGFF cannon blew up inside its circular magazine in the Bf109s right wing. Despite handling difficulties Neumann was able to nurse his aircraft back to Guines airfield.

Above right: A map allegedly showing all Luftwaffe attacks against targets in England during the night of 24 August 1940. Such maps were handed out to the press in Germany and occupied European countries.

Right: On 11 October 1941 Major Lützow received the Eichenlaub mit Schwertern to his Ritterkreuz after he had obtained 89 victories. He was the fourth member of the German Armed Forces to receive this award. Here, Lützow is being congratulated by Hitler. Lützow almost survived the war but was killed on 24 April 1945 while flying a Messerschmitt Me262.

were attacking. My eyes wandered towards the front of the formation again. Nothing was happening there . . . or could those black specks be enemy fighters? To be certain I reported my sightings over the radio. The Jagdgruppen tensed up as they waited for a frontal attack.

'Yes, there they were! They thought that our bomber formation was least defended in front. They dived from high above us — one, two, three, six, a complete Staffel. Now it was time to do something. I dived towards the first one and fired away.

'My bullets hit him and he went down in front of the bombers. The others followed him for security. At the high speeds we were flying there was a big danger of a collision. This attack had been fought off, but already a new English Staffel was coming from the right. It tried an attack from the side — nothing doing, we turned towards them. Our machine guns shot down one after the other. All around us smoke trails floated through the sky. It was a fantastic sight.

'Then one of them dived at me. He had broken off his attack on the bombers thinking that I was a better target. We rushed at each other and I saw flames flickering from his eight machine guns. Instinctively I ducked but my eye stayed on the gunsight and my fingers gripped the stick ready to push the button. We were speeding towards each other, neither of us altering course. For a fraction of a second I wondered which of the two of us would give way and in the next moment the Englishman roared over my cockpit within centimetres.

'I yanked my machine around, back towards the bomber formation. It was still well protected but those aircraft flying below were they all Messerschmitts? I gunned the engine and dived. Just below the foremost Kette there were some fighters. Something seemed to be wrong. One of the bombers veered away from the formation, leaving a long white smoke trail. Dammit. I flew towards the bombers at full speed, then I saw: they were English two-seater fighters — Defiants.

'Unseen they had approached the bomber formation from below and were now firing into the defenceless bombers with their four machine guns. It would cost them dearly. I got to within 30m of the first one and my guns spoke — a volley, and a flame flickered around the enemy's fuselage. Debris flew away and suddenly fire erupted everywhere. Slowly he fell off on one wing — that one wouldn't be coming back. Then I went for the next one. A tight left turn with the throttle wide open and I was already close behind him. I pushed the button and he too started to burn and fell away to the right. My last bullets hit his left wing. A large piece came away as if cut off with a razor blade. He too had had his fill, I did not have to pursue him. But there was yet another one. He had seen his danger and dived to the right. I followed him and was at his neck at once. After the first burst of fire his four machine guns pointed upward. The gunner had been hit. Get on with it, fire-fire-fire! But my ammunition was spent. I had to let him go. With a long black smoke trail he disappeared downwards. I turned away sharply, back to the bombers.

'In the meantime, the formation had dropped its bombs and turned away to the east. But then all hell was let loose. The sky was black with AA bursts. The bomber formation flew on. They knew that only one thing would help them: to fly on, straight on course, with an iron will. And the English attacked again.

'This time they came from above — each time a single aircraft which scurried through the bomber formation, passed through all of us and disappeared below. Woe to the German aircraft that was disabled. It had to veer away from the formation and either became the prey of the English fighters that lay in wait or had to crash land on enemy soil. Sometimes it managed to stagger to the Channel, hoping that the *Seenotdienst* would help. This service picked up crews often, sometimes right before the eyes of the fast English launches and many times also shortly before dark.

'I flew towards the *Führungskette* of the fighter formation and reported that I was leaving. The pilot waved at me in a friendly way. Once again everything went well. I ordered the Gruppen to land. Many aircraft flew over their airstrip waggling their wings before they landed.'

Above: This Bf109E of 2/JG52, W Nr 5184, has its first victory mark painted on.

Right: Dramatic photograph showing Leutnant Landry of Stab I/JG3 dying despite the care administered by his captors. He had been shot down by Plt Off Down, flying a Hurricane of No 56 Squadron over the Thames Estuary on 28 August 1940. Landry flew Bf109E-5 (W Nr 0941). Among the spectators who saw Leutnant Landry being shot down, was Winston Churchill, who was visiting the defences of the south-east at that time. *Fox Photos*

500th Victory

On 1 September 1939, World War II started. Exactly one year later ZG76, the Haifisch-Geschwader (Shark Geschwader) obtained its 500th victory over England. From the spring of 1940 its commander was Oberstleutnant Walther Grabmann, a veteran of the Condor Legion. This is how a war correspondent saw the Geschwader's 500th victory:

'At the battle headquarters, the adjutant was busy recording the Geschwader's victories. He counted them once, then again and finally looked over his figures for a third time: "Up to today we have got 483 confirmed kills," he reported, smiling. The commander was rather astonished at the high figure — the Geschwader had set out against the enemy so often, done its duty and shot down everything that could be shot down, but had not been too interested in victory scores. "483 victories in one year — amazing how it mounts up," He said; then his eyes lit up: "We're on another mission today. Let's push ourselves and get to the 500th. It would really be something if we could manage that."

'Two hours later the wing was ready for take-off. Everyone knew what the commander wanted. The 500th had to come down.

'When we met the bomber formation we had to cover, the tension mounted. We hoped the Englishmen were going to be coming as well. Circling around the bombers we approached the British coast. A number of Messerschmitt fighters joined us. Down below the green-blue sea reflected the sun's rays. Small cumulus clouds dotted the sky; visibility was good.

'When we crossed the coastline no fighters appeared. We covered half our journey and had still not met any opposition; usually we met enemy aircraft above their coast, but today we and the bombers approached the target unmolested. Then something flashed in the sunshine far below us. Were we mistaken? No — a large formation of English fighters could be seen clearly and they were preparing to attack us.

' "Fighters coming at us from the front," was rapidly reported by radio to all our Zerstörer. Our first Gruppe, led by the commander, attacked the English formation. The latter dispersed and dived through our ranks, getting away without firing at our bombers. After they had regained some height they tried to assemble again but didn't succeed because the first German Zerstörern were already among them. The commander attacked the foremost British fighter and both machines fired at each other head on. After a few seconds the Spitfire was finished and it crashed down, burning. A second suffered a similar fate. A third was attacked by the adjutant and this battle too was soon over, and another Englishman bit the dust.

'But the British were tough. Again and again they tried to break through our defensive circle. But the scene remained unchanged. A Zerstörer left the circle for a moment and a rash Spitfire went down. The hot combat went on for nearly half an hour . . .

'In the meantime the bomber formation, accompanied by two other groups of the Zerstörergeschwader, reached its target, an airfield near London. Just as the bombers prepared to release their bombs, a number of Hurricanes came diving out of the clouds. At any cost they wanted to disperse the bombers and hinder their attack — but then they were met by the Zerstörern. The formation was able to drop its bombs unhindered. Most of them fell on the hangars and barracks, some on the edge of the field where a

Left: Oberstleutnant Walter Grabmann, Kommodore of ZG76 and Generalmajor Theo Osterkamp, Jagdfliegerführer 2. Osterkamp was awarded the Pour le Mérite on 2 September 1918, as leader of a Marinejagdstaffel. He was one of the very few pilots to fly fighters in both World War I and II. During World War I he obtained 32 victories and he got a further six at the beginning of World War II. *via Grabmann*

number of aircraft were standing. We could observe the results clearly and took pleasure in the fact that our sortie had not been for nothing. While the bombs were being dropped, the Englishmen had gathered again and time after time tried to get at the bombers. Their tactics were clear — to avoid battle with the fighters and Zerstörer and to attack the bombers. But they did not succeed. Watchfully the Zerstörer stayed near the formation and as soon as a Hurricane showed up in the vicinity several "Haifische" (sharks) went after it . . .

'The English pursued us until we reached the coast where they stopped. Above French soil we said goodbye to the bomber formation, which had not lost a single machine, by waggling our wings. Now our thoughts turned to our victories. Had the Geschwader obtained 17 kills? Had we reached the magic figure of 500? Our Gruppe had shot down seven. We hoped the other groups had the missing 10.

'After landing tension mounted at the Geschwadergefechtsstand. At last the telephone rang. The Kommandeur of the second Gruppe reported six victories. Splendid! But we still needed four more. Then the long-awaited call from the third Gruppe came through. Anxiously everybody looked at the Kommodore who held the receiver to his ear. When he said four, all faces lit up and everyone present shouted an enthusiastic "Hurrah".

'Proudly the success was reported to the General. Exactly 500 victories in one year of the war — and the Haifisch-Geschwader would keep it up.'

The claims made by the Luftwaffe pilots right after aerial combat were later carefully examined and only those seriously substantiated were confirmed. Many times it became clear that the same victory had been claimed by several pilots. It was then credited to only one pilot.

Walter Grabmann, a Bavarian born in 1905, later rose in rank to become a Generalmajor and Divisionskommandeur. He survived the war after flying a total of 237 missions, of which 137 were made during the Spanish Civil War. His victories totalled 12, six in Spain and six during the attack on France in 1940.

Above left: At the end of August 1940, Generalfeldmarschall Albert Kesselring, commander of Luftflotte 2, visited ZG76 at the Abbeville airfield. From left to right: Generalfeldmarschall Kesselring, Oberstleutnant Grabmann, Kommodore of ZG76, Hauptmann Groth, Kommandeur of II/ZG76, Hauptmann Liensberger, Kommandeur of V (Zerstörer) LG1 and Hauptmann Kaldrack, Kommandeur of III/ZG76. Besides Kesselring, only Walter Grabmann survived the war. Erich Groth was killed in action on 11 August 1941 near Stavanger, Horst Liensberger was shot down on 27 September 1940 by Plt Off Leary of No 17 Squadron near Maidstone and Rolf Kaldrack, a former Condor Legion pilot, was killed, as related before, on 3 February 1942.

Centre left: A scene at Laval, France, during the first half of September 1940. From left to right: A Feldpolizeiinspektor of the Geheime Feldpolizei der Luftwaffe (Luftwaffe Secret Field Police), Hauptmann Schascke, adjutant of Stab/ZG76 giving advice to an Oberleutnant of ZG76 in leather flying combination and his wireless operator. Schascke later shot down 15 aircraft during the Russian campaign but afterwards failed to return from a mission.

Bottom left: Impressive front view of a Messerschmitt Bf110C-4 of ZG76. At left, between some trees, a Dornier Do17P-1.

Above and centre right: These two Bf110C-4s, coded M8+CP and M8+EP, of 6/ZG76, willingly posed for the camera. RAE pilots who had occasion to evaluate the Bf110 in flight found that 'the Bf110 was a very pleasant and safe aeroplane for normal flying but its handling qualities left much to be desired, owing to its lack of manoeuvrability at medium and high airspeeds'.

Bottom right: Daily maintenance of a Bf110C-4 of ZG76.

Right: Bf110s on their way with towering clouds forming an impressive background.

Below: Photograph taken from the cockpit of a Bf110 of ZG76 on 9 September 1940. The specks in the distance are actually 15 Heinkel He111's of KG1 'Hindenburg' on their way to London.
via Grabmann

An Occupied Airfield

From an early date, Antwerp ranked as one of the world's very few cities that could boast three fully equipped aerodromes. In 1909 hangars had been erected at the Wilrijkse Plein, a military training ground south of the city, just outside the fortifications. After Antwerp had been bombed by the brand new LZ25 Zeppelin on the night of 24/25 August 1914, a few aircraft of the Royal Naval Air Service were stationed there and it was from that airfield that the first raid by British naval aircraft on objectives in enemy territory took place, when on 9 October 1914 Sqn Ldr Spenser Grey tried to attack the German airship sheds at Cologne. Unfortunately he failed to find them due to fog, but Flt Lt Marix, flying aeroplane No 168 (a Tabloid) had better luck and was able to destroy LZ25 in its shed at Dusseldorf.

Wilrijkse Plein was taken over by the Germans when they conquered Belgium, and during World War I the airfield was used by German military aviation. When the war ended it was used as Antwerp's official aerodrome until 1922, when it was closed down and replaced by the airfield at Deurne which was better placed to serve the city, being only 4km from the city centre.

A year after the Wilrijkse Plein airfield had been opened, Baron Pierre de Caters, holder of the FAI Flying Brevet No 1, opened his

Below: A Dornier Do17Z-2 of II/KG3 in its revetment at Deurne airfield. Note 7.92mm MG15 machine gun in the lower part of the glazed nose, an unusual position. The lettering on the entrance door reads *ZURÜCK, Um dem Motor herumgehen, Von hinten einsteigen.* **(Go BACK, Go around the engines, Enter from behind).** *Bundesarchiv*

private airfield at St Job in 't Goor, 15km north-east of Antwerp's city centre. A rich owner of a chateau and large tracts of land, he did not hesitate to have an airstrip cut through some of his woods. He put the fully equipped aerodrome at the disposal of his fellow pilots of the Royal Belgian Aero Club. The airfield was not used after World War I.

A third airfield, 15km NNE of Antwerp, was built in 1911 by the Belgian Army on the large artillery range at Brasschaat. It is still in use today.

However, most important of Antwerp's early aerodromes was Antwerp/Deurne, which is still in use today as Antwerp's main airport. Deurne had nothing to do with Belgium's Aéronautique Militaire/Militaire Luchtvaart or, indeed, military aviation in general, until 1939. In March of that year, the military came to Antwerp/Deurne, even if only in the form of the 3rd Escadrille of the Flying School at Wevelgem. Wevelgem airfield had become too small to handle the expansion programme of the Belgian Aéronautique Militaire/Militaire Luchtvaart, and Deurne had been chosen as an overspill airfield. Commander of the 3rd Escadrille was Capt Danckers and it was equipped with Avro 504s. November 1939 saw more military aircraft stationed at the airfield; some 10 Fairey Foxes of 1/I/1 (First Escadrille of the First Groupe of the First Regiment). This unit had been detached to Deurne to be nearer to the 4th and 5th Army Corps, stationed along the Albert Canal.

While the interwar years saw little military aviation at Antwerp/Deurne, it was connected by regular services to the other cities in Europe and many sports aircraft visited the airfield. On 16 May 1934, two Focke-Wulf 'Stieglitz' and two Heinkel 'Kadett' biplanes landed. The aircraft had aboard a party of 10 German sports flyers on their way back from a visit to England. Among the party were Staatsrat Florian, the Gauleiter for Dusseldorf, Flieger-kommodore Loerzer, President of the DLV (Deutscher Luftsport Verband) and Flieger-Kommandant von Bülow. The Battle of Britain would see General Bruno Loerzer commanding II Fliegerkorps and Oberleutnant Harry von Bülow commanding JG2.

On 10 May 1940, shortly after dawn, 36 Luftwaffe bombers of KG4 attacked Deurne. They were too late — all Belgian airworthy military aircraft had left Deurne 20 minutes earlier for the comparative safety of the auxiliary airstrip at Hingene, 17km further to the south-west.

On 19 May the German 18th Army marched into Antwerp, only hours after the airfield had been 'destroyed' by the retreating Belgian Army. A number of explosions had cratered the airfield but these demolitions could not prevent Messerschmitt Bf109s of I/JG26 landing there on 23 May, five days before the capitulation of Belgium. The pilots were billeted in Antwerp hotels. Among other missions, they flew against RAF fighters at Dunkirk. This was the case also on 1 June, the day they left for airfields nearer to the frontline in France. Other units equipped with Bf109s replaced them.

During the first days of the occupation Belgian civilians were free to come and look at the Bf109s in their revetments. They were not allowed near the aircraft but from an adjoining railway embankment one had a good view of the rakish fighters. But then things changed. The author, 10 at the time, clearly remembers being chased away by a German guard with a fierce looking alsatian. Few Geschwader stayed in Germany, most of them were deployed behind the front. KG3 was ordered to the north of Belgium.

KG3 was already an experienced Geschwader. It had flown missions during the Polish Campaign — at the crossing of the Weichsel at Dirschau, at Graudenz, in the Bzura-pocket, at the

Top left: Ammunition for the MG15 machine guns has arrived.

Centre left: An SC250 bomb is being loaded on a truck with the help of a *Heuschrecke* (grasshopper).

Bottom left: Mechanics working on the port Bramo 323P, nine-cylinder, air-cooled engine of a Dornier Do17Z-2.

Right: Armourer cleaning the barrel of a 7.92mm MG15 machine gun.

Below: Gruppe Finsterwalde's first casualty during the Battle of Britain was this Dornier Do17Z-2. During a mission on 9 July 1940 the aircraft was damaged by a pilot of No 257 Squadron over Kent. With one dead and one wounded crew member aboard it crashed near Stabroek, some 15km north of Deurne airfield. *Archives J. Dillen*

crossing of the Natew, near Praga, Warsaw and Modlin. During the campaign in the west it had aided the German Army when it crashed through the positions of the Belgian and French Army in southern Belgium, in the Ardennes, at the crossing of the River Meuse, when pursuing the French Army, by attacks on airfields near Paris, by attacks against Dunkirk, Ostende, Zeebrugge, Torhout and generally aiding the German Army at the Southern front up to the Swiss border.

Geschwaderkommodore of KG3, the Blitz-Geschwader, was the monocled Oberst Wolfgang von Chamier-Glisczinski. He decided to base his Geschwader, part of II Fliegerkorps of Luftflotte 2, equipped with Dornier Do17s, on three Belgian airfields. The Geschwaderstab and II Gruppe were to be based at Antwerp/Deurne; I Gruppe at the former Belgian Air Force auxiliary airstrip Le Culot, 10km south of Leuven (this airfield was also called Hamme-Mille and is now the BAF Base Bevekom); III Gruppe went to Brustem, near St Truiden. Eventually a fourth Gruppe would be formed during the Battle of Britain at Chièvres, 45km SW of Brussels.

So II/KG3, Gruppe Finsterwalde came to Antwerp. Its Kommandeur was Hauptmann Otto Pilger. He had already visited Deurne airfield at the end of May. Pilger had learned to fly in 1928 and 1929 at the DVS in Schleissheim and had joined the Reichswehr in April 1929. His flying was limited to a 14-day training period every year until 1933 when he was trained as a fighter pilot, first at the Jagdfliegerschule in Schleissheim, later at Aviano in Italy.

From October 1933 till June 1934 he was clandestinely trained as a bomber pilot while flying the nightly Lufthansa route between Berlin and Königsberg. Then he joined Kampfgeschwader Boelke at Fassberg and the next year became a Staffelkapitän of II/155 at Leipheim. Next, he went to the Luftkriegsschule at Wildpark-Werder where he was active as a teacher of tactics. This activity was interrupted when Germany marched into the Sudetenland. In April 1940 he became commander of II/KG3. In 1978 he reminisced:

'When I first visited Deurne airfield in May 1940 no other Luftwaffe units were stationed there. As it was then, the airfield was barely large enough to permit daylight operations by the Do17 — but the airfield was enlarged after we had started operations.'

Left: Dornier Do17 crew getting ready for a bombing mission. Note that they wear their flying suits *over* their life-jackets. If the air-bottle was out of order, they could always blow into the black tube to inflate the jacket.

Below: A rubber dinghy is loaded aboard a Dornier Do17Z-2.

The peaceful Antwerp airfield now became Fliegerhorst 208/XI of the Luftwaffe and on 8 June the first of the 40 Do17Zs of II/KG3 arrived from Laon airfield in France. Gruppe Finsterwalde (Finsterwalde had been their peacetime garrison) had come to Antwerp.

During the night of 4/5 June, the RAF bombed the airfield and to help fill in the craters the Germans enlisted the help of some of the numerous unemployed from the Antwerp area. These civilian workers were also employed to built revetments all over the airfield. Many varied technical activities were also necessary to render the airfield suitable as a bomber base, and soon Luftwaffe specialists were laying power- and telephone-lines, placing warning lights on top of high buildings that surrounded the airfield etc.

All houses in the vicinity of the airfield were commandeered by the Germans and their occupants had to vacate them within 48 hours. These houses were then used to billet Luftwaffe troops. Small streets near the airfield were used to stockpile bombs. The airfield was surrounded by a brick wall that connected the houses, along the perimeter of the area occupied by the Fliegerhorst. Pillboxes for machine guns were constructed along this wall so as to be able to defend the airfield. Many tall trees that might hamper bombers while taking-off or landing were cut down and preparations were made to enlarge the airfield. As at every Luftwaffe bomber station, the necessary personnel and offices were installed to make missions possible.

At the heart of it all was the *Gefechtsstand* where the orders were given out. There was the *Kartenstelle* (map room) where each mission was prepared and the *Wetterstelle* (meteorological office). There was also a *Funk- und Navigationsoffizier* (wireless and navigation officer) who advised the crews. Very important was the *Bodenleitstelle* (ground control centre) which was constantly in touch with the wireless operators on board the various bombers so that the crew could be advised of important matters like changes in the weather. On the other hand the Bodenleitstelle was kept informed of the course of the action so that, if need be, the Gefechtsstand could issue new orders.

This Bodenleitstelle was operated by the Luftnachrichten-kompanie which came under the command of the Geschwader-kommodore and was responsible for all telephone and wireless communications between the Geschwaderstab and the various

Gruppen on one side, and between the Geschwaderstab and the higher echelons on the other side. All navigational aids were also the responsibility of the Luftnachrichtenkompanie.

Responsible for orderly take-offs and landings was the *Start- und Landeaufsichtsoffizier*, while the *Platzsicherung* was responsible for the security of the airfield.

The *Flughafen-Betriebs-Kompanie* with a strength of some 150 officers and men manned all posts to keep the station and its bombers operational. Three FBK working parties of some 30 men each kept the bombers of each Staffel operational and consisted of one *Zugführer* (troop leader), 12 *Flugzeugmechanikern* (aircraft mechanics), two *Motorenschlossern* (engine mechanics), one *Feinmechaniker* (for the instruments), six *Waffenwarte* (armourers), six *Bombenwarte* (bomb armourers), two *Funkwarte* (wireless mechanics) and one *Fallschirmwart* who took care of the Staffel's parachutes. More mechanics were available for minor repairs to the bombers.

Thirty-eight years later, Pilger remembered:
'The Gruppenkommandeur was responsible for everything in his Gruppe, for training, missions, technical availability of the aircraft, discipline and so on — all this according to the standing rules of the Luftwaffe. He was also responsible for the orders that were given only to his Gruppe.

'The Gruppe received the order for every attack from the Geschwader, either in writing, by telephone or even from person to person. Exceptionally, a special order could be given directly to the Gruppe from a higher echelon. These orders had to be worked out individually for each Gruppe. For each attack, time of take-off, the order in which the take-offs took place, and emergency airfields had to be worked out, and meteorological cover and intelligence had to be organised. In the case of attacks by the Gruppe alone, arrangements had to be made for fighter cover. Rendezvous points and times had to be agreed on in advance. This was usually done personally with the leader of the fighter unit whom I visited at his airstrip. In the case of large scale attacks which had been organised by a higher echelon like the Luftflotte or the Fliegerkorps, we only had to organise the take-off time and order, and the meteorological aid.

'For every Gruppenkommandeur, the technical side of it all was a daily worry. A maximum number of aircraft had to be serviceable. To make sure of this, often unconventional channels had to be followed besides the normal supply of reserve parts. For

80

example: the Do17's engines had exhaust flames that were barely visible during daylight but which stood out clearly at night. The Eberspächer firm at Esslingen on the Neckar had developed effective flame dampers which were a matter of life or death for us.

'These flame suppressors had to be delivered to us through the normal channels which, as our experience showed, took a long time. For this reason, my technical officer, Oberleutnant Breu, repeatedly flew to Stuttgart to get the flame suppressors directly from the manufacturer, without knowledge of the Generalluftzeug-meister and probably against the wishes of the latter. The flame suppressors were then installed in our aircraft by our own ground crew.

'Another example: every aircraft heavily damaged in battle and which had to be taken to rearward repair depots, had to be delivered with its complete equipment and armament. Due to our experiences of the first days of war, we had installed in our aircraft, besides the front and rear armament, two more machine guns that could fire laterally. Our need for MGs was therefore double that normally the case. We delivered the damaged aircraft to the rearward units without any machine guns and claimed that they had been wrecked completely and could not be repaired. In this way we always had the necessary reserve to equip all of our aircraft with four machine guns.

'Contact with other Gruppenkommandeure was very loose because of the distance between the various groups. For the actual attacks such contact was hardly necessary. However during meetings at the Geschwaderstab experiences in battle were exchanged.

'II/KG3 was often visited by prominent superiors. Oberst von Chamier, who lived in Antwerp anyway, often was at the Gefechtsstand. Whenever he participated in an attack, he started from Deurne. Generalfeldmarschall Kesselring also visited the Gefechtsstand and the various Gruppen frequently. General Loerzer only visited us once. At one time Generalfeldmarschall Milch was with us for a few hours. Of course Generals of the Army and of the Luftwaffe landed at Deurne in their liaison aircraft to go farther on in a car. However they did not call on me or visit our Gefechtsstand. I never had anything to do with the Fliegerhorst-kommandant. Any questions that arose and had to do with him were automatically handled by my Adjutant, Oberleutnant Lemme or my Verwaltungsbeamte Rg Insp Haudel.'

Later on, a paved runway would be built by a collaborating entrepreneur and the spire of an Antwerp church, situated on the axis of the runway, torn down. But before this, Gruppe Finsterwalde flew its first bombing mission against the English on 8 July 1940, five days after the RAF had issued its Operations Instruction 38 of 3 July which said: 'The enemy are using airfields and landing grounds in France, Belgium and Holland ... the intention is to destroy as many aircraft as possible on the ground thus forcing the enemy to withdraw.'

But before the RAF could mount any significant attacks on Luftwaffe airfields, higher priority targets appeared in the form of barges and other shipping concentrating in waterways in Belgium and Holland and it was not until September 1940 that the RAF made any significant attacks on Deurne airfield.

The Gruppe's Dorniers were over England on 9 June but this day suffered their first Battle of Britain casualty when Sergeant Forward of No 257 Squadron attacked a Do17 over Kent. The pilot got away and crash landed his aircraft at Stabroek north of Antwerp but one of the crew had been mortally wounded.

Missions against targets in England now followed in rapid succession. After the raids, the Do17s often had injured or dead crew members on board and it was not unusual for some of the

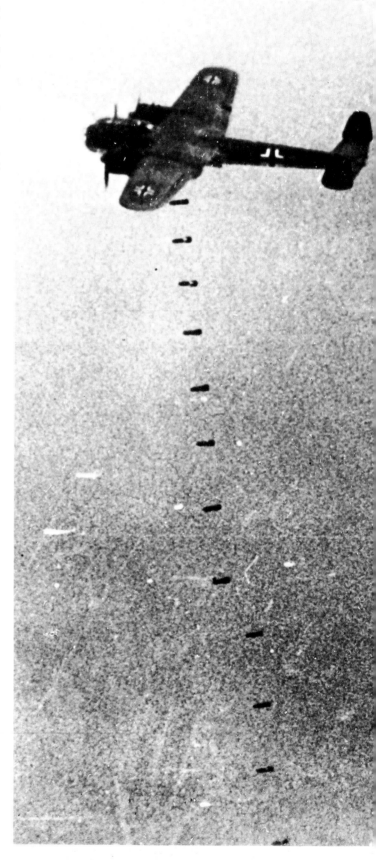

Left: Dornier Do17Z-2 unloading its deadly cargo.

Top right: The *Bodenleitstelle* (ground control centre) was in constant touch with the bombers.

Centre right: On the way home some bombers ask for a bearing that will bring them back to their base. The *Peilgerät* is being operated by one of the *Horst-Spezialisten*, a *Wehrmachtsbeamter*.

Below: Inside a Dornier Do17Z-2, turning on finals for Deurne-Antwerp airfield.

Perspex panels to be red with the blood of the unfortunate wounded. When badly wounded crew members were aboard, the aircraft usually stopped after landing and did not taxi towards the revetment until the casualties left by ambulance.

On 15 August the complete KG3 led by Oberst von Chamier-Gliscinksi flew against England again. III Gruppe attacked Eastchurch while the Stabskette and I and II Gruppen bombed Rochester airfield and the Short Bros Factory. On its way back the Gruppe reported that they had hit the factory and that they had observed smoke and fire. What the crews did not know was that they not only had destroyed six factory-fresh Short Stirlings, but that they had retarded delivery to the RAF of this vitally needed four-engined bomber by more than three months.

In September, the RAF began hitting back at Gruppe Finsterwalde. On the nights of 4/5, 14/15 and 17/18 they attacked the Deurne airfield but did very little damage. It was during this period that the Gruppe sustained the heaviest losses it would have during the whole of its Battle of Britain operations.

On 15 September the complete Gruppe was ordered to attack targets in or near London. When the formation reached Dungeness (which the German pilots referred to as *Dünnschiss*, a vulgar word for diarrhoea) it was attacked by 20 Spitfires and remained under constant attention of RAF fighters all the way to London. Harassed, the bombers dropped their bombs at random before trying to escape at full speed. Six of the Dorniers that had taken-off that morning from Deurne airfield did not return, having been shot down by RAF fighters.

Gruppenkommandeur Hauptmann Pilger himself had a very narrow escape. He recounts:

'During one of the last large-scale daylight attacks, before the Luftwaffe started to bomb London by night, the complete Gruppe attacked the Beckton Gasworks, east of London. Immediately after dropping my bombs, my aircraft received a direct hit by AA fire. Most of the cockpit and the instrument panel was destroyed, the glass of my sun-glasses was splintered — only the frame of my spectacles stayed intact and probably prevented worse injury — and the tube of my oxygen mask was destroyed. As I couldn't see anything my aircraft fell away from the formation, even if it remained fully controllable. In this situation, my observer,

Above: On the airfield anxious eyes follow the returning bombers.

Left: 'My aircraft received a direct hit from AA fire. Most of the cockpit and the instrument panel were destroyed. The glass of my sunglasses splintered . . .'

Above right: Many of the Do17Z-2s that returned had received hits from AA guns or enemy fighters. The crew always took a great interest in the hits 'their' Dornier had received.

Right: This Dornier Do17Z-2 of 6/KG3 is being manhandled into Hangar B at Deurne airfield. While the control tower was on the main building, Hangar B was on the other side of the airfield. On 29 August 1940 this same Dornier, coded 5K+FP (W Nr 3480), collided with a radio mast during a combat mission and crashed killing Leutnant Zein and two other crew members. *Bundesarchiv*

Left: This Dornier Do17 even returned with a defective rear tyre.

Below: A *'Sanitäts — Ju'* (ambulance Junkers Ju52/3m) has arrived to take some of the wounded home.

Right: Frequently Do17Z-2s of II/KG3 did not return to Deurne/Antwerp, having been shot down over England. This one, 5K+LM (W Nr 2669), lies burning on Folkestone Beach after having been shot down by a Hurricane of No 310 Squadron on 31 August 1940. Its crew, consisting of Oberfeldwebel, Lange, Unteroffizier Kostrpetsch, Feldwebel Berndt and Feldwebel Wunsche, were taken POW.

Below right: Two members of the crew of 5K+LM under guard. In the rear is Oberfeldwebel Lange. *Fox Photos*

Oberleutnant Laube, pulled me sideways out of the pilot's seat, sat himself at the controls and flew the aircraft back to Antwerp, at a height of some 2,000m. Laube did not have a pilot's licence, but had a very long experience of flying as an observer and had made a few "black" landings — meaning without permission!

'I was taken to a hospital in Antwerp where I was X-rayed and the blood and splinters were taken out of my eyes, face and upper body. As I had apparently only sustained flesh wounds and my vision was not impaired, I took command again of my Gruppe. Later on, Oberleutnant Laube obtained his flying licence but remained an observer. As such he was shot down over Russia in a Junkers Ju88.'

During the night of 15/16 September, as members of II/KG3 sat mourning their fallen comrades, as if to rub salt in their wounds, 15 Hampdens of No 83 Squadron attacked invasion barges gathered in the port of Antwerp, only a few kilometres distant. The pilot of one of the Hampdens was Guy Gibson while the wireless operator/air gunner of another was Flt Sgt John Hannah who later received the Victoria Cross for his valour during the attack on Antwerp when his bomber was set on fire. This young Scot was the youngest-ever recipient of a VC for aerial operations.

One of the pilots whom members of II/KG3 were mourning was the Staffelkapitän of 5/KG3, Hauptmann Ernst Püttmann, whose 5K+DN was shot down by Sgt Holmes of No 504 Squadron. His aircraft crashed in the forecourt of Victoria station and to this very day, scars occasioned by the crash can be seen. Püttmann was not the first Staffelkapitän of II/KG3 to be killed as Hauptmann Kükens, Staffelkapitän of 6/KG3, had been killed a week before, when on 8 September his 5K+CL collided with 5K+GL above Ertvelde, 50km west of Antwerp.

Pilger remained Gruppenkommandeur until November 1940 when he went to the Luftkriegsakademie, but not before the night of 9/10 November when a pilot demonstrated dramatically that Deurne airfield was still on the small side for night operations with Dornier Do17s. In order to make a normal landing it was necessary to touch down right behind the threshold of the runway and many times the twin-engined bombers had to go around again. On this night the pilot of a returning Dornier, having touched down in the middle of the airfield, chose to go round again. Something went amiss, however, and the aircraft crashed into some houses near the airfield where it hung precariously while a rescue team tried to get out two badly wounded crew members. The only available light was a few hand-held torches. Their efforts were to no avail as both men died of their wounds shortly afterwards.

After Pilger had left, Gruppe Finsterwalde had the occasion to sample the joys of the English 'Starfish', code-name of the decoy fire sites, when they tried to attack Bristol on the night of 2 December 1940. Feldwebel Kirsch, a dorsal gunner aboard one of the participating bombers remembered more than 30 years later: 'The briefing was short and to the point. The whole Gruppe was to attack Bristol. The navigators started to calculate their bearings, the procedure to be followed when attacked by night-fighters was discussed, it was decided which airfield would be used when heavily damaged aircraft returned, which light signals would be used for landing, what radio frequencies were available to the Staffeln, and so on. Soon heavily laden Dorniers were waggling across the airfield like drunken ducks. A small signalling lamp from the tower instructed the pilots to take-off.

'Once in the air the Staffel assembled around 5K+AM which was leading. While setting a course for Ostend, the 5th, 6th and Stabsstaffel all took their station in the formation. Wireless sets were checked as were the special "Knickebein" receivers that were carried in some Dorniers. When we neared the coast all position lights were put out and the distance between the various bombers was increased to minimise the risk of collision. We were now flying so high that everybody was wearing oxygen masks. While the two engines were monotonously droning away and while the gunners were anxiously scanning the sky, complete radio silence was maintained.

'When nearing the English coast, a clumsy movement by the navigator made his maps drop from his lap and float between the seats of the pilot and the navigator. Over the intercom the navigator asked me to retrieve them, so I undid my straps and leant down to look for the maps. In so doing the pipe of my oxygen mask came loose without anybody noticing. Shortly afterwards I lost consciousness.

'Luckily the pilot noticed the something was wrong. The navigator climbed down and helped me, while the pilot took a quick decision and dived, jettisoning his bombs into the North Sea. Racing low over the water the lonely Dornier flew home. On the way back I recovered consciousness and by the time we landed I was fit again.

'It had been a close shave for me, however, as it had been for the inhabitants of Bristol. When our aircraft had approached the city a special detail of soldiers, trained for such actions, had lit several fires on the outskirts, imitating a city on the ground, to mislead our navigators. II/KG3 neatly dropped its bombs into a swamp and Bristol itself was spared. The next day, however, reconnaissance aircraft discovered that it was undamaged and a report was drawn up.

'As a result Göring was enraged and ordered a new attack.'

Gruppe Finsterwalde left Antwerp/Deurne a few weeks later in January 1941 when it went to Oldenburg, Germany, to re-equip with the Junkers Ju88, the Do17 being obsolescent. Gruppe Finsterwalde thus left Antwerp and it would not be until September 1973 that a handful of survivors of the Gruppe still 'commanded' by Otto Pilger, visited the airfield again, endlessly reminiscing.

Below: Oberst von Chamier-Glisczinski, Kommodore of KG3. His Geschwaderstab also was based at Deurne/Antwerp airfield.

Below right: A formation of three Do17s above typical English countryside, on their way to their target. Note the different style of Balkenkreuze.

Smoke Billows over London

Through faulty navigation, the Luftwaffe dropped bombs on Greater London on 8 August and again during the night of 24/25 August, even if standing orders by Hitler himself forbade such attacks. The following night the sirens wailed above Berlin — RAF Bomber Command was attacking Germany's capital!

The British bombers returned during the nights of 28/29 and 30/31 August, 31 August/1 September, and 4/5 and 6/7 September. This was too much for Hitler and Göring. On Saturday, 7 September, the Luftwaffe attacked London 'en masse'. For the Londoners a months'-long ordeal began, for RAF Fighter Command it meant some respite, enough to save it from annihilation. That Saturday was one of the crucial turning points in the history of World War II and most historians believe that Churchill's order to bomb Berlin and Hitler's reaction turned the tide.

What was the German public officially told during the first week of the attacks on London? The answer can be found in the daily reports by the OKW which were broadcast not only in Germany but also in the occupied countries.

OKW Bericht (OKW communiqué) of 7 September:
'On 6 September the Luftwaffe successfully bombed targets important for the war effort in the south-east of England, like the aircraft works at Rochester and Weybridge, the oil storage depots of Thameshaven and the airfield at Kenley. A great number of enemy fighters which took up the fight were shot down.

'Attacks by night were executed against maritime and aircraft industry installations. Heavy damage was caused in Liverpool, Manchester and Derby and also in some towns on the south coast. Off several British ports mines were dropped from the air.

'During the night the enemy again attacked the Reich's capital and caused some loss of life and property by aimlessly dropping bombs on non-military targets in the centre of the town. The Luftwaffe therefore has now started to attack London with strong

Below: Harbour installations under attack during a bombing raid on London. Bomb explosions can be seen on land and in the River Thames.

forces. Last night dock installations in east London were set on fire and heavily hit by high explosive bombs. There and in the oil storage depot of Thameshaven heavy fires were visible from afar.

'Yesterday the enemy lost 67 aircraft, 52 in aerial combat and 13 on the ground. An enemy aircraft returning from Berlin was shot down by AA fire north of Hanover and another one was shot down by night-fighters near the Dortmund-Ems canal. 24 of our own aircraft are missing.'

The first *Vergeltungsangriff* (revenge attack) on London was deemed of such importance that the same day the OKW issued a second communiqué:
'This afternoon the Luftwaffe attacked the port and city of London for the first time with strong forces. The attacks were carried out as a reprisal for the intensifying night attacks during the last weeks by the English Air Force against non-military targets in the Reich. One single huge smoke cloud is spreading out from the centre of London towards the Thames estuary. Reports so far show that 31 enemy aircraft were shot down in aerial combat. Six of our own aircraft are missing.'

The attacks against London were also the subject of the OKW Bericht of 8 September:
'The attacks of our Luftwaffe against targets in London of great importance for the war economy which started on the night of 6/7 September were continued on the night of 7/8 September with strong forces.

'These attacks are reprisals for the night attacks on residential areas and other non-military targets in the Reich's territory, which were started by England and have been intensified during the last weeks. The Reichsmarschall is personally directing the attacks from the north of France.

'Uninterruptedly more than one million kilograms of bombs of every calibre have fallen on London and in the port and industrial areas near the River Thames. Quays, merchant ships, docks, warehouses, power, water and gasworks as well as arsenals, factories and transportation installations have been hit and partly destroyed by the heaviest of explosions. Large fires are raging in the vicinity of the docks. Large numbers of fighters sent in advance cleared the way to London for the bombers.

'Further aerial attacks were directed against the large oil storage depots and dock installations of Thameshaven, against the explosives factories of Chatham and the airfield of Hawkinge. Besides that bombers attacked industrial and harbour targets in Liverpool, Manchester, Birmingham, Cardiff, Bristol, Southampton, Portsmouth, Portland and 10 other places.

'The enemy again penetrated Germany last night. One wave turned against south-west Germany and dropped single bombs which caused no harm. The other part of the British bomber force tried to steer for Berlin, as on former nights, but was forced to turn back or to drop its bombs prematurely by the concentrated defence in the west. Only in a church in Hamm did bombs cause some damage. In yesterday's fighting the enemy lost 94 aircraft. 26 of our own aircraft did not return.'

Postwar research showed that reality was different. The Luftwaffe were missing not 26 aircraft on 7 September, but 31; one Do215, one He115, two Do17Zs, two Ju88s, four He111s, eight Bf110s and 13 Bf109s.

The OKW Bericht of 9 September again mentioned the attacks on London:
'Despite the poor weather, bomber units continued the reprisal attacks against London on 8 September and the night of 8/9 September. Aerial photographs confirmed the strong effect of

the attacks up till today. At night the attacking units could recognise their targets from afar because of the continuing fires. Again bombs were dropped on dock and harbour installations, oil storage depots, gasworks, electrical works, and waterworks, as well as warehouses on both banks of the River Thames. Several airfields in the vicinity of Lincoln were also attacked. In the Firth of Forth a merchant vessel of 8,000 tons was badly damaged.

'British aircraft attacked residential areas of Hamburg at night. Several houses were hit, a few civilians wounded, the total damage was slight. Total losses of the enemy yesterday were 22 aircraft. Two of them were shot down by AA fire, the rest in aerial combat. Four of our own aircraft are missing.'

On this same day the DNB (*Deutsches Nachrichten Büro* — German News Agency) reported:
'German aircraft which flew over London this afternoon could still see many large fires along the River Thames, especially at Victoria Dock, near the West India Dock, in the Commercial Dock and to the south of it. In the Bromley gasworks a fire was seen to start.

Left: Major Alois Lindmayer, Ṣtaffelkapitän of 7/KG76, after returning from a bombing mission. On 21 July 1940 he was awarded the Ritterkreuz.

Below left: Burning oil tanks at Purfleet after being bombed on 7 September 1940.

Below: Heinkel He111H-1 droning over England on its way to its assigned target.

Below right: In the night between 10 and 11 September 1940 bombers of the RAF bombed Berlin, the Reichshauptstadt. Amongst other damage this crater could be seen on the Charlottenburger Chaussee. In the background is the famous Brandenburger Tor.

The region in and near the bend of the River Thames was still engulfed by a large sea of fire and, furthermore, fires were still raging at several places, like in the town area south of London Bridge, in Wapping and in other spots near the River Thames.

'German fighter and bomber units attacked the British capital towards evening, as soon as weather permitted, and dropped bombs of every calibre on the harbour and dock installations to the north and the south of the River Thames. Several new fires sprang up besides the old ones which now light up the banks of the river.'

On 10 September the OKW reported:
'Last night British aircraft again dropped bombs on places situated far away from military objectives. In Berlin, as in other cities, single homes were damaged quite badly. German bombers and fighter units continued their reprisal attacks against targets in the British capital that are of importance for the war effort.

'As far as the weather permitted, harbour and dock installations, gasworks, waterworks and electrical works as well as warehouses and large oil storage plants were covered by bombs of every calibre. Fires which were visible from afar showed the way for our aerial formations. Further aerial attacks hit some harbours along England's west coast and the east coast of Scotland.

'The enemy's losses yesterday amounted to 44 aircraft. Two of them were shot down by AA artillery, one by naval artillery, the others shot down in aerial combat. 21 of our own aircraft are missing.'

For their part, DNB reported:
'German bomber formations again attacked a series of military and industrial targets in England on 10 September and the night of 10/11 September. The main objective of the missions was London, where industrial centres and war important installations were bombed with success. On 10 September the alarm was sounded in the British capital six times before 22.00hrs, even before the German night attacks had started in earnest. For the rest extensive

reconnaissance flights were made in the course of the day which brought home valuable information about the operation results up till today and about new targets.'

On 11 September the familiar voice again boomed over many a loudspeaker in Germany:
'Das OKW gibt bekannt: Last night the enemy dropped bombs on several places in northern France, Belgium and northern Germany which, however, occasioned only slight damage. A few enemy aircraft succeeded in reaching Berlin and dropped bombs there. Fires broke out in numerous residential and commercial areas and in the centre of the town two hospitals were hit. In the diplomats' quarter some streets had to be evacuated temporarily due to danger of buildings collapsing. One bomb fell upon the Reichstag [parliament building], another on the Academy of Arts. Five civilians were killed, several wounded. The energetic intervention of security and medical forces as well as Berlin's own units, prevented many fires from doing further harm. Yesterday, important installations in the city and port of London remained the most significant targets of the German reprisal attacks. Many new fires joined the older ones. Besides this, other war-important targets, especially harbour installations, airfields and industrial complexes in the south-east of the British Isles were bombed.

'South of the Hebrides a bomber sank a merchant ship of 8,000 tons from a British convoy. During the combats over England, three of our own aircraft were lost. AA artillery and night-fighters each shot down one of the aircraft attacking Berlin. Naval artillery on the Channel coast shot down four more enemy aircraft.'

In its turn, the DNB reported:
'Wednesday, at noon, German bomber units again attacked targets in south-east England. In London several industrial and harbour installations were covered with bombs. In Port Victoria, at the mouth of the River Thames, a large oil storage plant was set afire. In the Spitfire works at Southampton hangars were damaged.

'During these operations several aerial combats developed during which 54 British aircraft were shot down. 18 German aircraft are missing. We have learnt subsequently that last night two more enemy aircraft, which had just dropped bombs on Berlin, were shot down by AA artillery and night-fighters so that the number of enemy aircraft brought down by AA artillery, naval artillery and night-fighters amounts to eight.'

On 12 September the OKW stated the following:
'During the night of 11/12 September British aircraft once again dropped high explosive and incendiary bombs on residential areas in north Germany — amongst other places in Hamburg, Bremen and Berlin. Many fires broke out and damage was done to houses and workers' quarters. Unfortunately casualties were 14 dead and 41 injured. Well aimed AA fire, disciplined behaviour by the population and the energetic measures of the aid services, prevented more damage to the Reich's capital and other cities.

'German bomber, fighter and Zerstörergeschwader continued their reprisal attacks on London by day and by night. Docks and harbour installations, which were brightly lit up by fires, gas and electricity works, an explosives factory and an arms works were badly hit. Further attacks in the course of the day were made against an aircraft works in Southampton, where six hangars were destroyed, as well as against oil storage depots at Port Victoria. Night attacks were flown against Liverpool and other harbours on the west and south coasts of England.

'In the mouth of the River Thames, bombers dived down upon a convoy and set fire to one destroyer and four merchant ships. Two further merchant ships were hit. During the attacks against London several bitter aerial combats developed, during which 67 enemy aircraft were shot down. During the night a further six British aircraft were shot down over German territory by AA artillery. Naval artillery shot down six enemy bombers on the North Sea coast and one other on the Channel Coast, so that in total the enemy lost 80 aircraft yesterday. Twenty of our own aircraft are missing.

'Bombers attacked the harbour installations and the quays of Dover, causing fires to break out. The AA artillery positions of Dover were also successfully attacked and the positions were hit.'

The OKW's report on 13 September:
'British aircraft, which penetrated north and west Germany during the night, did not succeed in reaching their targets. A few bombs dropped on residential areas and on a village and did little damage.

'During our own armed reconnaissance over the south of England bombs were dropped on industrial installations in London, Bexhill, Brighton and many other places. South-west of the Isle of Man, a merchant vessel of 8,000 tons was probably badly damaged. During the night of 12/13 September, bombers again attacked the harbour and dock installations of London and Liverpool and started new fires. British harbours were again sown with mines. One enemy aircraft was shot down, one of our own is missing.'

And the DNB-Meldung of that day:
'As is being officially reported, three aircraft have to be added to the enemy losses as reported by the OKW on 10 September, while our own losses have to be diminished by four aircraft which have in the meantime returned to their Geschwader.'

On 14 September the Germans heard this report by the OKW:
'Yesterday the Luftwaffe continued its reprisal attacks against London by day and by night, despite unfavourable weather conditions, and obtained numerous hits on docks, warehouses and industrial works. In various places fires broke out. Furthermore the Luftwaffe successfully dropped bombs on airfields, industrial installations, harbours and railways in south-east England.

'The enemy undertook a few short excursions towards Holland, Belgium and France and dropped bombs at various places without causing substantial harm. Due to the heavy clouds only sporadic aerial combats developed. Eight enemy aircraft were shot down by fighters and AA artillery. Two of our own aircraft are missing.'

The OKW communiqué of 15 September:
'Despite the cloudy weather, during 14 September and the night of 14/15 September formations of Luftwaffe continued the reprisal attacks against all important targets in central and southern England, especially in London. In the London area, the docks received hits. Liverpool Harbour and the rolling mills at Warrington as well as several airfields, communication installations and harbours in southern England were also successfully bombed.

'During attacks against convoys a merchant vessel of 8,000 tons was thought to be sunk north of Ireland. Over London some aerial combats developed which were successful for our fighters.

'At night single enemy aircraft dropped bombs in Belgium and Holland and also on small villages in the border region of western Germany and also on the only military objective, a military encampment. Seven persons were killed and 16 wounded. Material damage is insignificant.

'Four enemy aircraft were shot down by AA artillery, 25 more by fighters. Five of our own aircraft did not return. Oberleutnant Müncheberg obtained his 20th victory.'

Night Attack

Luftwaffe attacks during daylight having proved to be disastrous, attacks at night became more frequent. Here is how one of the first night attacks against London was experienced by a pilot of Luftflotte 2, flying a Heinkel He111.

'At an airfield in northern France, a nice summer's day had just ended. For the first time in weeks men of a bomber Staffel had had time to relax in the sun for a few hours. Mechanics and the rest of the ground crews, however, were extremely busy and had to work late into the night to prepare the aircraft for that night's mission. For this mission the heaviest bombs had to be loaded aboard.

'The briefing at the Gruppen headquarters finished. The Staffel's nightbirds stood before our tents, fully bombed and fuelled up. The commander's aircraft had also been rolled out of its revetment. Only a few minutes to go.

'Our "Monika" had already been revved up and its engines were now idling quietly. It was ready to take-off for England and everything which it needed had been loaded. The Chief Mechanic, a stolid Bavarian, climbed down out of the machine and waved his hand full of confidence as if he wanted to say: "Herr Leutnant, things can get started, the bird is OK. It will see you through and do its duty". Before I climbed into the kite, I shook hands with the mechanic. In this gesture lay my gratitude, my appreciation for his constant attention to the machine. The lives of all the crew members hinged upon the conscientious work of these men. They were our true helpers, and we really stuck together.

'Equally admirable was the spirit of comradeship of our crew. Officer or simple soldier, Bavarian or Prussian, we were united by common experience, by common danger and by victories obtained together. More than 20 times we had flown across the Channel shoulder to shoulder.

'Today our target was the Albert Docks along the River Thames. While we were preparing ourselves, sitting in the cockpit, testing our oxygen masks and the wireless set, the observer said: "We'll pepper them tonight!"

'The sky that an hour ago shone with starlight had in the meantime been covered with clouds. While the machine roared across the airfield, the engines wide open, everything surrounding us was pitch-black — lights around the perimeter only lit up for a few seconds. Then we were completely surrounded by darkness as the perimeter lights went out, and the aircraft flew into the night. In

Right: Night has fallen, the crew of this Heinkel He111H-1 gets ready to fly a nocturnal mission.

Left: The nose gunner at his station.

Below: With the pilot and co-pilot standing on their seats, a Heinkel He111H-5 starts to taxi over the airfield.

Bottom: With flames belching from the exhausts, this Heinkel He111P-1 is about to start its take-off run. The Staffelkapitän, standing on his seat, gives the take-off sign.

Right: One aircraft after the other is coming in to land after a nightly attack, some of them with wounded or dead crew members aboard.

the cabin it was so dark that one couldn't see one's hand in front of one's face. Only the instruments glowed dimly.

'Cloud base was at 1,000m. At first we kept slightly below that and only now and then skimmed through tattered cloud fragments that hung somewhat lower. The hammering of the engines resounded into the night. We were flying against England! We roared across the Flemish countryside towards the Channel. It was not hard to orient oneself. Indeed, we had flown over this area so often by day, that we felt at home over it by night as well, added to which the navigator was steadily fixing our exact position. Short sentences over the intercom kept the crew in touch with what was going on.

'Unfortunately, tonight we couldn't see the high white breakers along the coast — the steep chalk cliffs of the southern coast of England were also covered by darkness. A cold draught tore along the left side of the cabin. The machine flew unsteadily and the flight was not exactly a very cosy one. We were thrown about constantly by the turbulence.

'From far away we could see the light of fires scattered over southern England. Burning industrial installations? Factories that had been bombed? Did the English really think we were stupid enough to think that. They were, of course, faked fires to divert us. My observer knew all those tricks. We compared our instruments, clocks and maps and continued on to the British capital.

'In order to be able to approach silently and without being disturbed, we climbed through the cloud cover. The altimeter went up by hundreds and thousands. We connected our oxygen masks and soon felt the wonderful refreshment that the oxygen brought. Far above us hung the deep blue star-studded sky with the half moon. Our aircraft approached the metropolis along the River Thames above silver-lined cloud mountains. To our right and to our left, in front and behind, we knew that other aircraft were heading for the same target even if we couldn't see or hear them. We got closer and closer to the city of millions. We didn't need a signpost because suddenly the clouds below us opened in a tremendous hole, through which we could see the earth. Already the searchlights were there to greet us. One after the other reached for us, now nearer, now farther away, until at last they had us locked in their beams. The cockpit was completely bathed in light and the aircraft next to us suddenly became visible as if it was daylight. One could read a map, so glaring was the light. For a moment we looked at

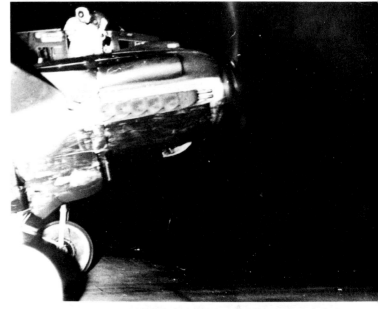

each other, "What a mess", shouted the observer, "let's get out of this light as soon as possible".

'Already the AA shells were flashing around us in a wild dance, one ball of fire after the other. I could hear one of the crew murmuring in the intercom, "The usual AA-waltz". The volleys began to come faster and closer to us. Even if we couldn't hear the report of each shell, even if we couldn't see the grey-black smoke bursts that surrounded us, we could feel that we were in the middle of the nightly bombardment by the rocking of our aircraft. It was a really heavy barrage trying to force us away.

'With a sharp movement I pushed the machine's nose down, dived some 500m, put the machine into a few sharp turns and we were out of it. The crew breathed a sigh of relief, but the respite lasted only a minute at the most — and then they had caught us again, and again let loose at us. The nearer we got to London the grimmer things got. The air space all around the town seemed to be armoured. I glanced at my watch, we should be above London now, although strong winds could have retarded us a few minutes. Everybody aboard was looking downward tensely.

' "We're there!" the aircraft's commander shouted quickly. We couldn't see very much of the metropolis, especially not of the outer limits — not that it was pitch dark below! On the contrary! What impressed us most at this moment during our flight was the sight of a metropolis burning in so many places. The Staffel before us had taken care of the necessary illumination.

'Even at the height of 5,000m, the glow of the fires was still dazzling, a grim sight — tens, no hundreds of fires, too many to count. Everywhere flames were flickering, everywhere sparks were flying. It looked as if the sea of houses was covered with fire — a unique vision.

'One could imagine hearing the explosions in the factories, the bursting of the gasworks, the wailing of the sirens, the clattering of broken glass, the roaring of the flames and the hollow sound of buildings tumbling down. How those millions must be trembling in their cellars. However, we were thinking about the riches that had been amassed since time immemorable along the many kilometres of the River Thames in huge warehouses, wheat silos, oil reserves — everything that England now needed in large quantities for war. And then there were the formidable docks which the island kingdom needed for its indispensable merchant navy. Even at 5,000m one had such thoughts on seeing the burning capital. At the same time I thought of my costly bomb load which I'd dragged across the Channel . . .

'We got lower and lower. We could see the water of the River Thames glimmering in the dark. We saw the immense estuary and also the characteristic curves of the river along which so many targets were situated. We could see the moon reflected in the water of the river. My observer cursed and cursed again. He wanted his target right in his sights, even in the thickest hail of fire. Sometimes it was really unnerving how he risked everything to be sure to get his target — he could really have got the devil out of hell. All the while we felt the umistakeable shuddering of the explosions below us. The AA artillery was breathing down our necks and time after time the dazzling light of the searchlights lit up the aircraft.

'Then there was an explosion and we received our first hit and a few pieces of shrapnel whirred through the fuselage. A large hole appeared right in the middle of the aircraft and the wind howled through it. The machine must have received other hits. "Bad shooting," the observer shouted, "they won't get a second chance". Our "Monika" was still flying and both engines were working normally. We'd been lucky again.

'Now I had to listen attentively to any order from my Franz (navigator bombardier) and had to trust fully to his judgement. Once again tracers flew towards us and crashed through the cabin. There was a deafening noise; instinctively all the crew ducked together. Then it too was over and we smiled at each other. "Courage, Johann, we will get through." The commander always found the encouraging word which enabled one to forget all danger. One's position could be hopeless but he would never lose his sense of humour. Again and again he rallied the crew together, when anything threatened to go amiss. In serious moments one only had to look at his face. All the crew was convinced that things couldn't go wrong with our "Monika".

' "Can't you smell anything, lads?" The Oberleutnant cried out unexpectedly. He sniffed and sniffed. I controlled the fuel system, and looked to the left and to the right of the engines sniffing the air as well. Dammit, he was right. The kite reeked badly with an evil smell of burning. "I can't find anything, our machine seems alright" I cried back. "I've had the smell in my nostrils for some time, but I didn't want to say anything," the mechanic reported.

' "But what can it be, it certainly isn't our bird."

' "Well then, it must be the smell of London burning," the

commander answered calmly. And we learned later he was right; other crews had made the same observation.

'I thought that we must have reached the target by now and that the Albert Docks would get their plastering. But no, our commander thought differently. Again he asked for a left turn. He had to be sure before he let loose; he did not want to be distracted by the fires of the docks that had already been hit. He wanted to see the target he had memorised right in front of him.

' "Now!" he yelled suddenly. "Now we're right. Bomb doors open." We were flying straight at the docks, but we were bloody low. It was totally unthinkable to let the bombs go from this height. From second to second I waited for an order. We had to get a few hundred metres higher, throwing those heavy bombs from this height went against all the rules. But my good old Franz had a different opinion again. He knew how important it was to hit such a significant target with a full load of bombs.

' "Attention, I am dropping the bombs!"

' "I hope things turn out alright!"

'But the Oberleutnant trusted his special guardian angel, and we all thought the same thing — why should we get hit?

'For the rest of my life I will be proud of those minutes in the enemy's hell above the Albert Docks. Every flight against England required courage, determination, deliberation, cold-bloodedness and skill in avoiding the enemy's AA artillery and fighters. Of course, avoiding action was out of the question for us now. The observer had no use for zig-zagging during his bombing run, even when AA artillery shells flashed by like many coloured arrows. On the bombing run, one had to clench one's teeth.

'Suddenly I heard, "There they go!". Both our heavy bombs tumbled down into the whirlpool of fire that was the Albert Docks. A jolt went through the aircraft. Suddenly the steering became lighter — one felt it had become many hundreds of kilograms lighter. I span the machine round to let the observer had a look at his target. The gunner and the wireless operator stared down tensely as well. All of us wanted to live through these seconds. We all wanted to witness our success and be able to report it to our comrades in the Staffel back home.

'We were turning through AA shell fragments and without knowing it, received more hits. But it was not so bad now. Our "Monika" would surely get back home. Unfortunately we could not see anything of the falling bombs in the darkness. We could imagine them tumbling head over tail as they hurtled down and bored themselves into the target. We turned back and set course for home. Not a single minute was to be wasted unnecessarily. We did not know what lay in wait for us in the dark. As we turned away we looked down for a last time on the flickering fires of the metropolis.

'I would like to have been a gifted painter and to have been able to retain this vision on canvas. And I thought about the large target map at the Flugleitung, which we always saw when we started against England, the map with the many target points.

'Soon after leaving London the AA fire got lighter and less accurate. Our aircraft flew on unmolested. The wireless operated reported our success to the base and then started to unwrap his chocolate calmly. I thought about doing the same — after all, having been through all that nerveracking business my stomach deserved something. But that day the devil seemed to have had a hand in the play. Suddenly the wireless operator cried out in an excited voice whilst throwing away his chocolate "There, a shadow behind us — probably a night-fighter".

' "He must be mad! He's seeing ghosts!"

' "No, Herr Oberleutnant, I can see the machine clearly. A British night-fighter."

' "Night-fighter? Not that as well!"

' "Dive away immediately," the commander ordered. Indeed we had to get away as soon as possible, and I pushed the machine's nose down. I dived with every horsepower we had, but the Tommy overtook us to the left and shot yellow and red flares. What did he want?

'We found out very quickly. While we were diving we saw that the English searchlights that had been groping for us the whole time, were suddenly switched off so that everything around became very dark. "Monika" gave everything she had but the British fighter was faster than our bomber and already the eight muzzle flashes were flickering. It was sitting right behind our tail and the tracers whipped past the cabin, now to the left, now to the right. The situation was decidedly ticklish. At the same time, however, our own machine guns were hammering away and their aim wasn't too bad. Our gunner fired straight at the muzzle flashes of the fighter whose pilot seemed to be an excellent marksman. Then he peeled away to his left, apparently having been hit, because the next second there was nothing to be seen of him. He must have thought that shooting down an He111 would have been easier.

'The AA artillery, however, accompanied us until Dover. "Good shooting," our Oberleutnant called out. In the meantime we had left the English south coast behind and I flew towards France contentedly. The night had become quiet and lighter. We would be able to land in about 20 minutes. The commander once again sent out a report. Everybody aboard was in a good mood.

'In the middle of the Channel I suddenly noticed the left engine was not functioning properly. I reported this to the commander. It started to splutter. Convulsions ran through the aircraft and from minute to minute the jolting became more pronounced.

'Surely the engine had been hit. The oil pressure diminished slowly but steadily. I hoped the kite would see us through until we crossed the Channel. Dammit, we did not want to end up as prisoners-of-war in England, and we certainly did not want to take a cold bath at night.

'Then it happened. The left-hand propeller stopped completely and the aircraft nosed downwards until I trimmed it. The flight engineer came forward from his seat in the fuselage and cut off the fuel for the dead engine, pumping it to the other one which now had to work twice as hard. Everyone was on his guard, each minute saw the tension mounting.

'The mechanic had his doubts: "I wonder if we'll be able to land? At night on one engine it will be tricky!"

' "Leave that to me," I answered.

'We got lower and lower and our speed built up. Fortunately we were able to cross the Channel and set course towards our airfield. The flaps and undercarriage went down. Everybody waited anxiously for the aircraft to touch down. A last circle around the base and then the machine glided towards the illuminated landing strip. The small stars of light which showed us the way quickly became large lamps — the machine was already gliding across the warning lights. Now we had to lose height rapidly. The last 20 metres . . . it seemed an eternity before we reached the ground. But then the machine jolted, not very softly, bounded up once and then sank back to the earth again. We'd made it in one piece.

'The aircraft rolled towards the hardstands where we were greeted warmly by our comrades. They had expected us much earlier and hadn't received our broadcasts. Indeed we now established the wireless set had been inoperative. Then we all stood together and looked at our aircraft. We were amazed, it had received dozens and dozens of hits. The chief mechanic stroked his machine as if to say: "You have done an excellent job," while our Oberleutnant told the story of the flight.

'After a handshake we left each other to rest and get new energy for the next day. Already the first Staffeln were flying above us with roaring engines on their way for a dawn attack.'

A Vociferous Visitor

A frequent visitor to many Luftwaffe units participating in the Battle of Britain was Hermann Wilhelm Göring, a Bavarian born in Rosenheim, who was Reichsminister for Aviation and Supreme Commander of the Luftwaffe.

During World War I he had been a dashing and daring fighter pilot but in World War II he lacked all the qualities of character and knowledge needed to lead a formidable force like Germany's Luftwaffe in to battle against a well-equipped and strong-willed opponent. Indeed he lacked any knowledge of strategic, and for that matter of tactical, air warfare, believing, like most of the high-ranking Nazis, that a strong will was more effective than a knowledgeable mind.

When, in early September 1940, he visited JG26, its commander Major Galland, had the following to say, which he wrote in his book *Die Ersten und die Letzten* published in 1953 by Schneekluth Verlag at Darmstadt:

'A fortnight later we met the Reichsmarschall again. This time he came to visit us on the coast. The large-scale attacks of the bombers were imminent. The air supremacy necessary for these had not been achieved to the degree expected. The English fighter force was wounded, it was true, but not beaten. Our pursuit Stuka and fighter force had naturally suffered grievous losses in material, personnel and morale. The uncertainty about the continuation of the air offensive reflected itself down to the last pilot. Göring refused to understand that his Luftwaffe, this sparkling and so far successful sword, threatened to turn blunt in his hand. He believed there was not enough fighting spirit and a lack of confidence in ultimate victory. By personally taking a hand he hoped to get the best out of us.

'To my mind, he went about it the wrong way. He had nothing but reproach for the fighter force, and he expressed his dissatisfaction in the harshest of terms. The theme of fighter protection was chewed over again and again. Göring clearly represented the point of view of the bombers and demanded close and rigid protection. The bomber, he said, was more important than record bag figures. I tried to point out that the Bf109 was superior in attack and not so suitable for purely defensive purposes as the Spitfire, which although a little slower, was much more

manoeuvrable. He rejected my objection. We received many more harsh words. Finally as his time ran short he grew more amiable. He asked what were the requirements for our squadrons. Mölders asked for a series of Bf109s with more powerful engines. The request was granted. "And you?" Göring turned to me. I did not hesitate long. "I should like an outfit of Spitfires for my squadron." After I had blurted this out, I received rather a shock. It was not really meant that way. Of course fundamentally I preferred our Bf109 to the Spitfire. But I was unbelievably vexed at the lack of understanding and the stubbornness with which the command gave us orders we could not execute — or only incompletely — as a result of many shortcomings for which we were not to blame. Such brazen-faced impudence made even Göring speechless. He stamped off, growling as he went.'

Right: Reichsmarschall Hermann Göring during a visit in Northern France, briskly walking to a Gefechtsstand.

Left: Everywhere Göring went, his two personal standards went with him. Left: *Standarte des Reichsmarschalls des Grossdeutschen Reiches.* Right: *Kommandoflagge des Reichsministers der Luftfahrt und Oberbefehlshabers der Luftwaffe.*

Below left: Having a chat with a young Luftwaffe member. Behind Göring is General Bruno Lörzer, commander of II Fliegerkorps.

Below: Göring talking to a Feldwebel who has just returned from a mission. Note the special swagger stick carried by Göring: it was made of ivory with gold and platinum fittings and with a black/white/red twisted cord with tassel.

Right: Sampling the food of 'his' men.

Below right: Everyone but the Feldwebel seems to enjoy Göring's joke. Note again the Reichsmarschall's standards.

Below: Looking across the Channel towards England. He would never get there . . .

Right: A 'fully equipped' Reichsmarschall looking at a map that has been 'adjusted' by a wartime censor. At left are Bodenschatz and Kesselring.

Bottom: From left to right: General der Flieger Hans Jeschonnek, Luftwaffe Chief of Staff; General der Flieger Bruno Lörzer, Commander of II Fliegerkorps; Reichsmarschall Hermann Göring; Hauptmann Berndt von Brauchitsch, Gruppen-Kommandeur of IV (Stuka)/LG1, son of Walther von Brauchitsch, Supreme Commander of the German Armed Forces.

Galland's 40th Kill

On 24 September Maj Galland shot down his 40th victim. How this came about was told by Maj Hermann Kohl of the Staff of Luftflottenkommando 2:

'Only yesterday the 38th and the 39th *Abschusstrich* (victory marks) were painted on Major Galland's Bf109. Would he bring home his 40th victory today? Everybody at the landing strip seemed charged with high voltage, the whole Geschwader awaited its commander's return with confidence. He would certainly have done it if the British had been kind enough to keep their appointment. The Geschwader was on its way to London, covering bomber formations flying deep into the heart of Britain. The weather gods were well disposed and the bomber formations succeeded in getting to their targets and dropped their bomb load

with success — but it looked as if the British fighters were not in a fighting mood that day. High in the sky everything was calm and peaceful.

'Maj Galland scanned the sky continuously. Surely they would let him have his fun today? Then things began to happen. Spitfires in close formation and some solitary Hurricanes came speeding in from a distance. They were many hundreds of metres higher than the German fighters and seemed to have another target in sight. Indeed, the formation suddenly dispersed and part of the British unit kept on its course. Maj Galland and his fighters were ready for the reception. As always it was only a few seconds before the formations met each other. Galland had already given his instructions: the British formation had to be dispersed. There was nothing to be done except to charge at the line of enemy machines. Galland zoomed upwards in his aircraft. He climbed steeply towards the Englishmen accompanied to his right and to his left by comrades of his Geschwader. His plan succeeded at once. The British dispersed and the dogfights began. Galland attacked the nearest one who did not succeed in getting away. No favours were given — a few well aimed bursts and the Englishman's destiny was sealed. Vivid flames shot from the machine, which flew through the air like a torch. It was a Hurricane. It started to spin, helplessly lost. It seemed as if the pilot was lost as well but no, at the last possible moment a black spot loosened itself from the burning machine and a parachute bloomed wide in the air. The Englishman had baled out.

'Maj Galland's comrades had a lot on their hands. For the Geschwader it was a successful day and they flew back to their airfield proudly. At the airstrip everyone was standing around watching the sky. The Adjutant and the Hauptmann beim Stabe were waiting with anxious confidence. Any moment now the commander and his fighters had to come back. Time and time again the possibility of a 40th victory was talked about — he had shot down 39 adversaries and had succeeded in getting away from the most difficult situations. Surely he must have scored this time with his usual calm and coldbloodedness. None of his men doubted his success for a moment. Then there they came, the Schlageter-

Left: Oberstleutnant Adolf Galland receives the friendly attentions of the 'Geschwaderhund', the squadron's pet dog.

fighters. All eyes were raised to the sky. Everybody wanted to be the first to spot the commander's machine. "Look, he's waggling his wings" everyone shouted and, yelling wildly, they ran towards the landing aircraft to receive their commander with their congratulations upon his fortieth. His eyes shone with joy at getting his kill. Everybody now wanted to shake hands with him. Galland was extremely beloved by his men, he was not only a hard tough soldier and fighter but at the same time an exemplary, kind comrade. His special greeting was for his personal mechanic: "We did it again today!" he said and then he fulfilled the intense wish of those standing around him by telling them briefly how the aerial fight had gone.

'In the meantime a mechanic was already at work with a brush. Forty victory marks on the tail! During the afternoon the congratulations of the Führer and supreme commander of the Wehrmacht arrived. Major Galland was ordered to Berlin to receive the Oak Leaves to the Ritterkreuz of the Iron Cross. The Führer wanted to hand them out just like he did to Mölders only a few days before . . . '

Right: During a hunting trip Galland and a fellow-officer enjoy some hot soup provided by a field kitchen. Note shotguns on top of the Mercedes-Benz '230' Kfz12 passenger car.

Below: Galland was frequently visited by all kinds of people. During early October it was the Japanese Ambassador in Germany, Oshima, who came to pay Galland a visit. From left to right are: Gen der Flieger Wimmer, Oberstleutnant Galland and Ambassador Oshima.

Above left: After receiving Galland's attentions, this Spitfire became one of his victims and another victory on his already impressive list.

Above: Oberstleutnant Adolf Galland in the cockpit of his Bf109E, after returning from a mission. Note the tension on his face, a sure sign of the strenuous aerial battle he has just been through.

Left: In a totally different mood, Galland has his boots attended to in a most unusual way at St Omer airfield.

This page: Christmas 1940 a 'notorious' visitor came to JG26 'Schlageter'. The photographs depict Hitler being welcomed by Galland on arrival and 'waved-out' on departure.

Sinking the
Empress of Britain

Twenty-six year old Oberleutnant Bernhard Jope from Leipzig loved to fly. He had yearned to do so as a schoolboy and had been taught with the DLV (Deutscher Luftsport Verband) at Königsberg in Eastern Prussia in 1934-1935. In the latter year he joined the Luftwaffe as an officer candidate, later to become a professional officer. Before World War II started he had already seen action in Spain, with the Condor Legion where he flew Heinkel He111s of K88 and he later also saw action in Poland and France.

On 26 October 1940 he readied himself to make his first operational sortie with 2/KG40 at the wheel of an imposing Focke Wulf Fw200C, an aircraft type which Winston Churchill would later call, with his usual rhetoric verve, the 'Scourge of the Atlantic'. At the same time Capt Charles Howard Sapsworth was looking forward to being home again in Edinburgh. Indeed the ship he commanded, the 42,348 ton *Empress of Britain*, flagship of the Canadian Pacific Company's fleet, was only some 150 miles off Ireland, on its way from Cape Town to Liverpool. The *Empress of*

Britain had 643 people aboard, including military families on their way back to England and a number of military personnel. The youngest passenger on board the heavily armed and camouflaged ship was 11-month old Neville Hart.

Capt Sapsworth had been in the service of the Canadian Pacific Company for 28 years, in fact before Bernhard Jope had been born. In May 1939 he had had the honour of bringing the King and Queen back after their tour of Canada and the United States on board 'his' *Empress of Britain*. Now, sailing without an escort, he had encountered good weather and was a day ahead of schedule. Little could he have suspected that within a few hours his ship would be a blazing wreck, the largest British liner to be sunk during the war, having been set on fire by bombs from Jope's four-engined

Below: Focke-Wulf Fw200C-3 of KG40 being readied for a flight.

This page: Photographs taken from Oberleutnant Jope's FockeWulf Fw200 Condor of the *Empress of Britain* after the ship had been hit.

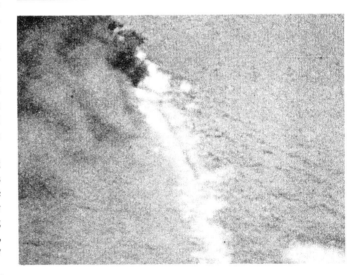

Focke Wulf Fw200C, a makeshift bomber developed from the elegant Condor airliner.

This is Jope's account of the flight, during which a Luftwaffe meteorologist was aboard, written shortly after he returned to his base at Bordeaux:

'At half past three in the morning my crew assembled and I announced our assignment: "Armed reconnaissance over the Atlantic, north-west and north of Ireland" and I discussed briefly the execution of this assignment in view of the weather and available battle reports. Only a few words were spoken and then we stepped outside the small briefing hut into the dark night. The aircraft's engine had just been tested and the mechanic announced that the machine was ready for battle.

'After a short salutation and then a few handshakes with people wishing us luck and good results we took our seats and rolled our heavy aircraft to the take-off area. It was four o'clock. The engines roared away, the machine left the ground and would only come back after 15 or 16 hours. Behind us the lights of the airfield were extinguished and everything became quiet again as if nothing had happened. Only our small community high up in the sky lived in tension and went on its long, lonely way towards the enemy.

'After a time no more words were spoken on board. The pilot watched his instruments carefully, because outside total darkness reigned: not a star, not a single light was to be seen. Soon we were above the coastline, the weather was not very friendly, and slowly the hours went by. Now and then we saw the faint light of a fishing trawler. Seven o'clock, eight o'clock, slowly the sky became lighter, the first signs of dawn could be seen and below us, water, only water.

'Far away to our right we could see the south-west coast of Ireland and its rugged mountains. We kept our distance because Ireland was neutral and we did not want to violate this neutrality. The flight continued north-westwards. The light was improving rapidly but time and time again clouds, large areas of rain and thundershowers hampered visibility. We reached the area where the English convoys tried to get through. We all watched the sea very carefully so that nothing would escape us. Suddenly one of my crew came rushing forward and pointed at a large ship to starboard — a big fish, he thought.

'And he was right. Three large funnels became visible through the grey of the drizzle. It was moving very quickly in a hurry to get

Above left: Jope after his successful mission being greeted by Major Petersen, Commander of KG40.

Above centre: Jope being congratulated by Major Petersen.

Left and above right: Jope posing for the photographers.

Below left: Jope being offered flowers by ground personnel.
Eckardt Brandt, son of PK Sonderführer Wilhelm Brandt who actually took the photographs.

to a safe harbour for protection against the bad weather. I gave a few short orders. Everybody was at battle stations, all weapons were tried once more and we made a wide circle, preparing to attack the ship from behind. Every crew member reported they were ready and I attacked. I dived down to 400m, 300, 200.

'Already the ship had started evasive manoeuvres and the whole might of its aft armament was brought to bear upon us. We answered this defence by firing back. Then we were right on the ship, 150m above it. Our first bomb had dropped and I banked sharply to the left to get out of reach of its defensive fire. There was loud cheering when the tail gunner reported a hit on the forward part of the ship. That the first bomb was a hit was of advantage to us because the ship had already started to burn and the fire was spreading rapidly. But the ship had also hit us and the bombsight had been shot away from the front of the nose. This wouldn't help it as I determined to loose off the remaining bombs by sight. I repeated my attack and once again tried to get behind the ship even if it was very hard to do so. Again defensive fire came up at us from all guns. The bullets glowed red — probably 4cm. Once more, we were right above the ship. The second bomb dropped. Unfortunately it was a miss.

'Immediately we returned and attacked again. I wanted to make it more difficult for them to fire back and decided to attack from the front where the ship was already burning fiercely. Furthermore, most of the defensive AA guns seemed to be at the back of the ship. Again I had to make a wide turn to get in front of it. At the same time we could hear the SOS signals it was sending out. But with only one hit we could not let it go as the damage wasn't bad enough to stop the vessel reaching port anyway. We made our third attack. I let go two bombs at the same time hoping that at least one would hit.

'One of the bombs was, indeed, a hit on the back of the ship this time. It was now burning both at the front and the back. All defensive fire had been silenced and the flames were spreading extremely rapidly. Smoke intensified and fire glowed from every window and hatch. Lifeboats were put into the water as staying on board the ship had become impossible, the heat unbearable. The ship was already listing. We wondered whether it would sink before our very eyes? But we couldn't wait any longer and its destruction was certain. It was lying motionless, abandoned by its crew, smoking, burning and immobile. For the last time we circled around our victim and then started the long way back. The fight had lasted over half an hour. The ship defended itself fiercely.'

Besides himself as pilot and commander of the aircraft, Oberleutnant Jope's crew consisted of: Lt Burkhardt, co-pilot; Uffz Dörschel, flight engineer; Uffz Iwang, first wireless operator; Ogefr Mix, second wireless operator and Dr Habich, navigator-meteorologist.

One of the Focke-Wulf's engines had been put out of action by AA fire from the *Empress of Britain* and the aircraft limped back on three engines, landing at Brest. Jope could only reach his home airfield at Bordeaux the next day after the engine had been repaired. The crippled liner was taken into tow but several U-boats had been alerted by a radio call from Jope's Fw200 and two days later it was given the coup de grâce by U-32, under command of Oblt z See Jenisch. Jenisch's U-boat was sunk in its turn on 30 October by HMS *Harvester* and *Highlander*.

A short time later Jope's commander, Oberstleutnant Edgar Petersen, gave him a transcript from the 29 October issue of the *Daily Telegraph* which contained an extensive report about the sinking of the *Empress of Britain*. From this report Jope learned that of the 643 people aboard, 598 had so far been landed at a western port by British warships. They included Capt Sapsworth

and 11-month old Neville Hart, who was saved by being lashed in a blanket on the back of a sailor who slid down a 60ft rope into a lifeboat with Neville slung behind him like a papoose. The newspaper went on to tell 'Neville was as contented as if he had been wrapped in his mother's shawl. He was wide-eyed with wonder at the novelty of his descent, but showed no signs of excitement. His parents, sister and brother were also saved.' For weeks on end Jope's victory was trumpeted in the German newspapers. With headlines like 'The Ship of the Plutocrats is no longer afloat'.

A prewar German passenger of the *Empress of Britain* sent him some photographs of the ship where extreme luxury had abounded and a publicity folder of the ship's 1936 World Cruise. 'All servants' rooms have telephone connections with master apartments', the folder said. Even the Focke-Wulf Flugzeugbau GmbH used Jope's feat for its advertisements. Indeed one of them showed a Fw200 in the air while below it an empty lifebelt from the *Empress of Britain* floated on the water.

Jope was rapidly promoted to Hauptmann and in December 1940 was awarded the Ritterkreuz. The *Empress of Britain* was not the last ship Jope would sink. Among others he sank the *Kapetan Stratis* on 22 January 1941. In 1943 he became commander of KG100 that successfully attacked ships with its Dornier Do217s which carried Fritz X and Hs293s. KG100 hit the battleships *Roma* and *Italia* on 9 September 1943, and later USS *Savannah*, HMS *Warspite,* HMS *Spartan* and HMS *Janus*.

In early April 1944 he was summoned to Berchtesgaden where Hitler presented him with the Oak Leaves to the Ritterkreuz but in January 1945 his KG100 was disbanded. He was then given command of KG30 which was preparing Beethoven operations, the codename for the explosive-laden Junkers Ju88s upon which a Bf109 or Fw190 was mounted.

After the war he studied engineering at the Technical College of Stuttgart and in 1955 joined the newly formed Lufthansa, flying Convairs, Super-Constellations and Boeing 707s until he was pensioned off in 1974 being relieved in the pilot's seat by his eldest son.

Thirty-nine years after attacking the *Empress of Britain* he reminisced about that particular flight and how its aftermath still had not finished:

'This event in my life has followed me until this day. Even now I regularly get letters from historians, authors and researchers. In many books about World War II and about the Luftwaffe my name is mentioned and time and time again I am asked about the attack and am asked for reports.'

Asked how he aimed the bomb that hit the *Empress of Britain* he remembered:

'The Lotfe 7D bombsight was an optical precision instrument designed for attacks on small targets from a certain height. Due to the large amount of fuel we had to carry, we could only carry two 500kg bombs or four 250kg bombs, so we had to drop our bombs one by one from a very low height. We did not have a bombsight to do so, therefore our mechanics made a notch and bead sight. The notch was situated in the cockpit just behind the pilot's windscreen and the bead was fixed on the nose of the aircraft. It was this bead that was shot away during my first bombing run towards the *Empress of Britain*.'

Left: Focke-Wulf Fw200 crew members were taught ship recognition with the help of metal models, which where also available to civilians as toys.

The first four bomber pilots mentioned in OKW Reports during the Battle of Britain

On 27 April 1940 Hitler ordered that from then on the names of soldiers and officers who had distinguished themselves in battle should be named in the OKW Berichte, but it was not until 27 September 1940 that a Luftwaffe bomber pilot taking part in the Battle of Britain was mentioned. However, after that bomber pilots were mentioned on four successive days:

27 September

'The crew of a bomber led by Hauptmann Storp distinguished itself in a special way during a courageous low-level attack in the centre of England'.

On 12 September 1940, Walter Storp became Kommandeur of II/KG76 and received the Ritterkreuz on 21 October for his attacks against the Rolls-Royce works in Coventry. He ended the war as commander of the 5th Fliegerdivision in Norway.

28 September

'During the attacks against central England a crew led by Oberleutnant Leonhardi distinguished itself in a special way. Despite heavy defensive fire it bore down on an armaments factory during a low-level attack and dropped its bombs in the middle of the target.'

25-year old Irmfried Leonhardi of Dresden was killed on 31 August 1941 while flying with 7/KG53.

Below left: Hauptmann Walter Storp.

Below: Oberleutnant Leonhardi with his crew; Leonhardi is second from left.

Above left: Major Harlinghausen.

Above: During the Norwegian Campaign, Major Harlinghausen attacked the SS *Sirius* in the Westfjord when the British Navy steamed towards Narvik. The Heinkel He111 flew so low over the ship that the tip of one of its masts became stuck in the aircraft's fuselage. Photo shows the tip of the mast embedded in the He111 after its return.

Left: Oberleutnant Dietrich von Buttlar in front of his Heinkel He111H-5.

29 September

'Led by Major Harlinghausen, a formation of bombers was able, on 28 September, to sink two merchantmen of a total tonnage of 12,000 BRT off the east coast of northern Scotland despite heavy AA fire from the heavily protected convoy.'

Oberstleutnant Harlinghausen was awarded the Eichenlaub of the RK on 30 January 1941, the eighth officer of the Wehrmacht to receive this award.

At the time of the mention he was Chief of Staff of X Fliegerkorps. Martin Harlinghausen became Chief of the Luftwaffenkommando West during the last days of the war and later served with the new German Luftwaffe until 1961.

30 September

'A very important armaments factory was attacked at low-level in the Midlands. A heavy calibre hit occasioned heavy destruction in the works. The attack was made by a bomber led by Oberleutnant von Buttlar.'

Dietrich von Buttlar, a Berliner, then belonged to 4/KG53. He was killed during the night of 7 May 1943 while flying a Ju88A-14 of I/KG6 against England.

Baling Out at Night

What it was like to bale out of a Dornier Do17 at night was recounted by an Oberleutnant who had bombed Portsmouth on a stormy night:

'We were flying our "Cäsar" towards Portsmouth, which we could make out from afar because of the fires. The Tommies put up a nasty barrage in front of us and I took evasive action to make the enemy gunners' job more difficult, diving and climbing continually. But then, suddenly, there was a loud explosion to port and then repeated crashes and crackles. We had been hit by some AA fragments but continued to fly towards our target that soon lay below, clearly visible. Rapidly we dropped our bombs and then turned sharply 180 degrees to the right.

'We had to get through the AA barrage again before turning towards the sea. We had just turned towards our base when the flight engineer suddenly shouted from the ventral step: "Machine on fire." Already I could see long, vivid red flames coming out from under the port engine. "It must be the oil line," the flight engineer said, "probably shot through". That of all things! That's why we had heard noises some time ago.

'Immediately we shut off the fuel lines and feathered the propeller. We were wobbling, badly rocked by the turbulence towards the Channel and the engine was still on fire. While I thought about the best thing to do next, the wireless operator tried to send out a message about the damage to our engine, but soon called: "Herr Oberleutnant, the FT-Anlage (wireless-set) is out of order, it's been hit as well."

'Dammit! What should we do now? Land on the water? I decided against that because in the darkness, in this horrible stormy weather and without being able to send out our position, this course of action would mean certain disaster. I decided, therefore, to fly on under any circumstances and my decision was strengthened by the flight engineer's opinion that it was possible to continue. He knew well what the engine might do but then I couldn't do otherwise even if we risked an explosion. We took the shortest route to the French coast.

'Either way it was a bloody risky situation. Fanned by the wind the fire got worse all the time and the machine was steadily losing height. We could see the foaming sea clearly in front of us, the waves whipped up by the wind. Above us, huge menacing dark

Left: Each Staffel had a *Fallschirmwart* (parachute packer) who was responsible for the Staffel's parachutes. These highly skilled men literally held the lives of the pilot or crew-member bailing out of his aircraft in their hands.

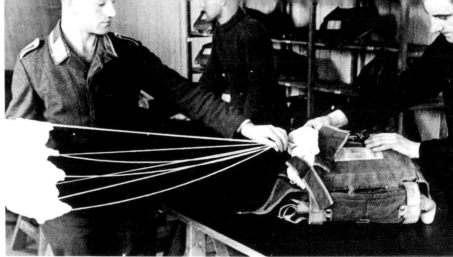

Right: The last item to go into the parachute container is the pilot chute. After pulling the ripcord this miniature parachute pulls the main chute canopy out of the pack.

Below: Even if a parachute was not used by the wearer it was repacked in the interest of safety. Here crew members are collecting their parachutes and have already donned their life-jackets. Note glasses worn by one of the crew.

Bottom: Flying at night was often made difficult by the blinding glare of enemy searchlights. When a pilot was caught in this deadly beam he had to take immediate evasive action in order to get out of this death-trap.

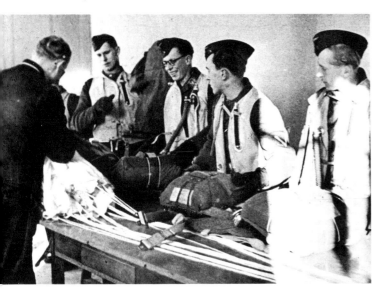

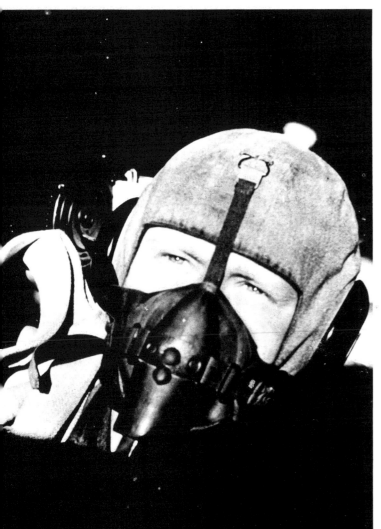

clouds towered up, around us there was a wild storm and the brightly burning torch of the port engine.

'After some time a dark mass loomed out dimly against the background of the water through a veil of fog. Land in sight! Our spirits once more were revived. It was the steep rocky French coast. The flight engineer kept boosting our spirits: just keep on flying! The right engine kept on doing its job, but was starting to splutter now and then. A few minutes later terra firma lay below us and the coast had been left behind. Everyone aboard breathed a sigh of relief. But we weren't out of mortal danger yet.

'To risk a belly-landing was totally out of the question, as the land was completely unknown to me and it was still dark. So we got used to the idea of having to bale out. We were very low and we tried to get higher — and slowly the machine climbed to 900m. That was it, however, and it would have to be enough. The flight engineer said that now was the time. Swiftly I trimmed the machine for horizontal flight and then shouted "Bale out!"

'With one hand I gripped the stick until everyone had got out. Then I eased myself out of the pilot's seat and let myself drop over the wing, slightly brushing the flaps. It happened as fast as lightning. Suddenly I felt a jolt, and then I was swaying like a clock's pendulum under the parachute, like a plaything of the storm. Soon I saw a dark red-shining mass swoop past. It was our "Cäsar" which, seconds later, came out of the grey cloud curtain going down terribly fast and crashed in a large ball of fire. While I was slowly sinking down I suddenly noticed under me a shadow getting lower and lower. An open parachute. With all my might I cried out: "Hallo hallo — who's there?" And from far away, like the voice of a ghost a reply resounded back towards me: "This is the flight engineer. And who's there?" "Here is the pilot."

'I had no time for further considerations as the earth was rushing up to me with great speed. Just as I was about to prepare myself to receive the shock, it was too late. I had slammed down, tumbled head over tail and was being dragged along by the parachute. Finally I managed to push in the lock and free myself of the harness. I found my flight engineer further on lying in a freshly ploughed field. Before he got there had been hanging on a tree until he was carried aloft again, raised above some power wires to be dropped on the field. We both had come down alive, we were saved! But where were the other two comrades, my observer and my wireless-operator? Shouting brought no result and neither did some searching. Then the two of us marched towards a neighbouring village where we were met by a German sentry who had seen the fiery crash of our machine.

'Unfortunately many telephone-lines had been destroyed by the storm and I was only able to report back to the Staffel during the late afternoon. I was very pleased to hear that my two other comrades were also alive and on their way. So we were home again. We only needed a new "Cäsar" and then we could fly towards England again.'

Bombing Coventry

During the night of 14/15 November 1940, the Luftwaffe started a new phase in the Battle of Britain. For more than a month London had been bombed every night, but now the Luftwaffe started a series of attacks against industrial and military installations in smaller British towns and cities.

The first attack was directed against the industrial city of Coventry. Bombers of nine different units took part in it and the raid lasted nearly the whole night. The industrial capacity of the city was drastically reduced but extensive slum areas between the various factories were also devastated. The 14th century cathedral was also demolished and the attack caused an outburst of public outrage.

Hours before, Prime Minister Churchill knew the raid was coming, but took the decision not to evacuate the city for fear of giving away the well kept secret that many German wireless signals were not only being intercepted but also decoded. This secret was only made public when F. W. Winterbotham published his book *The Ultra Secret* in 1975. Furthermore, it is very doubtful if a city like Coventry could have been effectively evacuated with only a few hours notice.

Several Kriegsberichter took part in the attack on Coventry, one of these being E. von Loewenstern, who later wrote this report:
'It was 14 November 1940. The order: Mass attack on Coventry! Coventry? The German crews searched their maps. What was Coventry? For a long time they had known the city housed an

Below: Crew of a Junkers Ju88 getting ready for a nightly mission.

Above left: Donning their parachutes. Note externally slung bombs under this Junkers Ju88A-5. The inner ones are SC250 and the outer ones SC500 bombs.

Above: The groundcrew turning the inertia starter. Two SC500 bombs are visible on the external bomb racks.

Left: A Junkers Ju88A-1 revving up its engines. Note the propeller arc illuminated by the airfield lighting.

Above right: Night flying demands full concentration of this Junkers Ju88 pilot.

Right: After the raid the first cigarette always tastes best.

Far right: The inevitable reporters are present and the crew has to relate their eventful flight for the listeners at home.

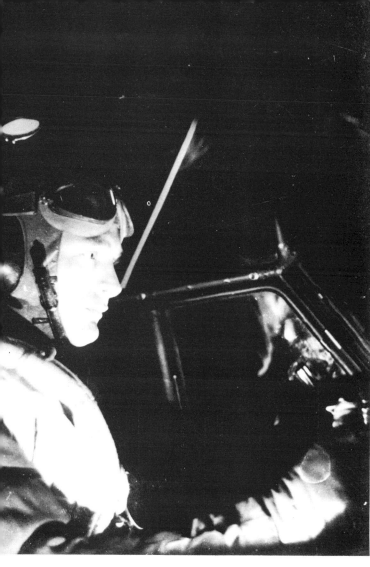

important centre of war production; but it was situated almost in the centre of England. Could the airmen find it in the darkness? The mission was discussed particularly eagerly.

'At midnight one heavily loaded aircraft after another took-off. "Right then. Hit them hard, Max!" the mechanic shouted at the wireless operator during a last handshake. Then we were off. The wireless operator sat in the passageway and tested his instruments. In the dark nobody spoke a word; but they all had the same thoughts: Coventry. Probably they would recognise it through the effect of the bombs of aircraft that had started earlier.

'Then suddenly the wireless operator pricked up his ears. He heard "Coventry is burning". And indeed one could perceive a glimmer on the horizon. "We are just above the English coast," reported the navigator, and a shining light could be seen in front. Coventry burning? The flaring signpost beckoned from the horizon. The burning industrial installations drew the airmen like a candle draws moths.'

The question 'Could the airmen find it in the darkness?' is rather ironic as the Kriegberichter must have known that the target was to be set on fire by a thousand incendiary bombs dropped by Heinkel He111s of KG100, even if he probably did not know that these Heinkels used the accurate X-Gerät as a navigational aid — but then he could not write such things in a report that was published in 1941. Another Kriegsberichter wrote this:

'Coventry — how often this city in the heart of England had been the target for single actions by our bombers — in good or bad weather! In the vicinity of this city and of its sister cities of Birmingham and Wolverhampton, many factories which were important for the English war effort had been hit during the last weeks. Here parts and engines for British fighters were being built.

'When we gathered at a briefing at the airstrip one night when the moon was full, we knew that our mission would have a special significance. Before giving all the necessary details about weather

Right: The groundcrew pushing back a Junkers Ju88A-5 in its dispersal area. Note exhaust flame dampers.

Below: Aerial view of Coventry after the attack. Bomb craters and industrial targets have been indicated. This, and the following photographs were distributed to the European press.

Bottom: The morning after ... This Junkers Ju88A-5's elevator has been badly damaged. The white swastika outline had been daubed over with black paint before the night mission as a precautionary measure against night-fighters.

and navigation, the Gruppenkommandeur explained in few but precise words our leaders' demands: this attack by virtue of its intensity must bring about a particular success for our air forces. A very exact bombing run by the pilot and careful aiming by the bomb aimer were to be of the highest importance on this mission.

'Our "Cäsar" was the first machine to sweep over the airfield, heavily loaded with bombs, and it set a course towards England. We all knew that a long and difficult flight lay ahead. Fortunately the storm — an unsympathetic companion during our last few nights' missions — had stopped. We approached the English coast with good visibility, very little cloud and only a spot of mist. Cities, rivers and canals were good signposts in this weather.

'At the coast, the AA artillery sent up to us our first greetings and searchlights feverishly flashed through the sky, but we kept to our course. Our first trial through the English flak was coming up; from far away we could see London's defensive circle. Other machines must have already visited the capital that night for we could see flashes of detonating bombs on the horizon. It had become quiet in the machine. In the cockpit the pilots were busy orienting themselves on the map with the aid of small torches. We were surrounded by the dark night. The searchlights and guns would only start again when the Midlands came into sight.

'Then came a cry of surprise — far to the north of us an enormous fire had broken out. Was that Coventry already? It was indeed our target — the huge fire must have been the work of our comrades who had flown before us. For minutes at a time many flares hung under their parachutes above the burning city. The vision became sharper as we approached: German bombs must have already wrought havoc in the target area. All conversation in our aircraft had stopped. We prepared to attack. Calmly the commander gave his orders to the pilot for the approach: "A little to the right, a bit more. Continue like this, now we are right."

'We got nearer and nearer. Dense smoke hung above the roofs of the town and was carried far away over the earth. Clearly we could see huge flames flickering ... Then we were over the target. The AA artillery fired desperately. All around us were the flashes of exploding shells. We could look right into the devastation, could make out clearly the large extent of the fires an see flames over large parts of the industrial city. In this moment our bombs were dropped. The machine jolted. Below new explosions caused a false daylight. We were the leader of a Gruppe of German bombers. Others had been before us, new ones followed — until the dawn of a new day which would uncover the total extent of the Coventry catastrophy.'

Birmingham Reconnaissance

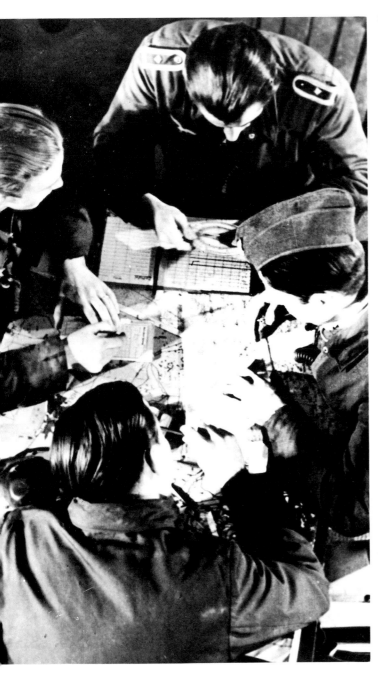

On the night of 19 November, Birmingham was attacked in the same manner as Coventry. The following day the Luftwaffe sent a reconnaissance Ju88 over the stricken city to take photographs to assess the damage, in order to prepare the next strike against Birmingham which was to follow on the night of 22 November. On board the reconnaissance Ju88 was Kriegberichter Hans Herbert Hirsch of LwKBK (mot)4. He wrote this report for the January 1941 issue of *Der Adler*:

'Once again we had received a mission order. Last night Birmingham had been the target of German Kampfgeschwader and aerial photographs had to be made of the effect of the attacks. The good old Ju we had used on our last few flights was in the repair workshop so we had to take another machine.

'Even during the outward flight the pilot noticed that the right engine was running unevenly, but he was a typical reconnaissance pilot and did not give up; he was determined to fulfil his mission. Then the city which had been hit so devastatingly the night before came into sight. Things were even worse here than in Coventry. Here the German Luftwaffe had hit harder than before. To rebuild the industrial installations of this city would take a considerable length of time — they had been flattened. The camera was running, picture after picture was taken, to give the information needed for the continuation of the assault. Due to the excitement caused by last night's catastrophy our reconnaissance aircraft's presence seemed to go unnoticed; only when the last photographs had been taken did small AA artillery clouds appear to the right and to the left.

'But the AA artillery seemed to have extended itself last night as all its fire was badly aimed. For a last time we flew over the centre of the city to get photographs of a large building complex which was still partly burning. Then the engine lost power again, and coughed as if it had a cold. The propeller pitch-setting was altered, the engine surged up, rpm dropped again, then the engine ran very slowly. There was no sense in continuing like that, so the pilot shut down the engine completely. We were left flying on one engine over Birmingham. We hoped no fighters turned up — the reconnaissance aircraft would have been easy meat now. But unharmed we flew over enemy territory towards the coast.

Left: A reconnaissance flight demands careful preparation. Each crew member has his own task to perform so that a safe flight to and from the target is assured.

'More and more the low and slow flying machine drew the attention of the AA artillery. Our Ju88 was flying through a veritable net of flak bursts which it was unable to evade with only one engine, and the fire got more accurate all the time. Now and then, when we were hit by shell fragments, there were rattling noises in the fuselage and wings. The altimeter needle steadily dropped lower. Suddenly there was a loud noise in the machine. A light AA artillery shell had slammed into the fuselage. Instinctively the observer gripped his parachute harness, but nothing happened, the aircraft continued flying. Near the coast there were two more such rattlings in the aircraft. The right engine, the source of all our troubles, lost its propeller and the radiator cover, and the right elevator came loose from the tailplane. Flying very slowly, losing height continuously and with a blocked elevator the machine reached the coast. Only a few more kilometres until our airfield.

'We had a last fright when the undercarriage would not extend — probably also damaged by shell fragments. It could not be lowered by hand either, so the pilot decided to make a belly-landing. Twice he had to go round again, then he landed. There was a hard jolt, the machine slid 50m on the grass, got caught by something and turned round twice. She looked bad but it would be possible to repair her. What counted was that valuable reconnaisance results had been brought home.'

Top left: A hand-held camera for oblique photography is handed out to a crew member.

Centre left: While another Junkers Ju88 has just landed a reconnaissance Junkers Ju88D is ready for take-off.

Bottom left: High above the towering clouds a lonely Junkers Ju88D is on its way to the target.

Right: As soon as the reconnaissance Junkers Ju88D has returned the photographs taken are evaluated.

Below: A photograph of Birmingham before the attack, handed out to the press. All important targets of a military or industrial nature have been indicated.

Right: Photograph of Birmingham after the attack.

Below: Photographs of the Rover Motor Works before and after the attack.

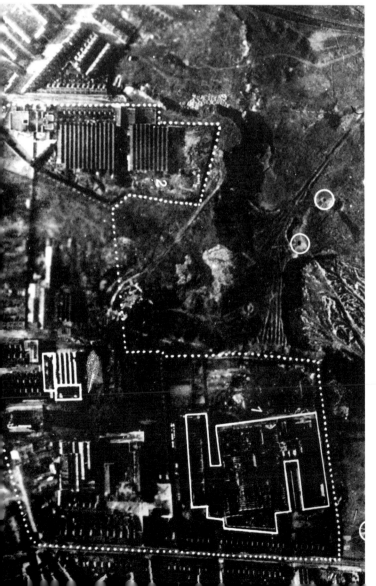

Towards another Battle

In February 1941, Jagdgeschwader 3 had been recalled to Germany to re-equip with the Bf109F. In May 1941 the Geschwader was back in France, at the airfield at Lillers, near Lille close to the Belgian border. Kommandeur was Hauptmann Oesau. Staffelkapitän of 7/JG3 was Oberleutnant Kurt Sochatzy. He recounts:

'In early June all ground personnel at our Staffel departed in an unknown direction. The orders foresaw catering for a 12-day land journey and an eight-day sea journey. Not a single goal corresponded with what we could imagine. Persia, Africa, India? Finally we gave up guessing.

'Two weeks later we too left Lillers, flying our Messerschmitts. Our destination: Strassburg (France, then Germany). Hauptmann Oesau told the Staffelkapitäne: "You will get further orders at every stopping place along the route." Every Staffel flew separately. After Strassburg we flew to Straubing on the Danube. After landing, I

Below: Lillers, May 1941. In the middle the Kommodore of JG3, Major Lützow and to the right Hauptmann Oesau, Kommandeur of III/JG3. In the background is a Messerschmitt Bf109F-2 with 300-litre drop tank beneath the fuselage. Many authors have written that this Rüstsatz 5 was only used on Bf109F-5 and F-6 types which appeared only in 1942 and this photograph proves them wrong. *Kurt Sochatzy*

walked towards the Flugleitung to get the next sealed letter. It flashed through my head how close Straubing was to Vienna. To visit my wife would take only a short trip — but our movement lay under cover of the strictest secrecy.

'On the letter which I got from the Flugleiter at Straubing was written "Staffelkapitän 7/JG3". I signed for the letter in the book. In front of the building I opened the envelope. Breslau-Schöngarten was the next airfield. This still did not disclose our final destination.

'We really enjoyed life in Breslau. They were joyful and restful days for us, young people. The people of Breslau were very friendly towards pilots. Nobody knew where our ground personnel were. Nobody knew when we were going further or where, except perhaps some of the many Staff officers whom we met in unusual quantities in town.

'Early on the fourth day we got a flight order and flight maps. The maps had been produced by the Militärgeographisches Institut in Vienna. The destination was Moderovka — a small spot between Krosno and Jaslo, near the German-Russian demarcation line. When I roared across the small airstrip at low level I could see our ground personnel below us, waving at us enthusiastically. I couldn't miss Bögel, my fat Spiess. He was waving a large white cloth violently. When I climbed from by Bf109, Buchholz, my chief mechanic, offered me a cigarette. I almost embraced him, so pleased was I that we were together again. The 7/JG3 was complete once more and a month later our Gruppe celebrated its 800th aerial victory.'

By 3 August 1941 Sochatzy had obtained 38 aerial victories and had destroyed 27 enemy aircraft on the ground. On that day he shot down a Russian Il-2 above Kiev but the enemy aircraft tore off his right wing and he had to leave his stricken Bf109. He was kept a POW for eight years, while in Germany he was officially declared dead. He returned to his native Austria in 1949 and now lives in Vienna.

Top: The ready room of 7/JG3 at Lillers. Nearest the camera, Leutnant Raich and to the right Leutnant Bayer. *Kurt Sochatzy*

Above: Oberleutnant Sochatzy, Staffelkapitän of 7/JG3 having a haircut during a calm moment. *Kurt Sochatzy*

Left: Early June, the ground personnel of 7/JG3 left Lillers. The photo shows a Hanomag SS100 (111), a Krupp 3-ton 6×4 (109); a Daimler-Benz LG 3000 (107) and an Opel Blitz. *Kurt Sochatzy*

Below left: The convoy with the ground personnel of 7/JG3 on its way towards an unknown goal, which would turn out to be Moderovka on the (then) border between Germany and Russia. *Kurt Sochatzy*

Last Victim of the Baby Blitz

A wreath was laid yesterday on the grave of a German Serviceman — with the blessing of the Brighton Branch of the Royal British Legion.

Mr Henry Brook, 82-year old vice-president of the branch and a veteran of World War I, performed the ceremony and spoke the Legion exhortation over the grave in Bear Road cemetery. The ceremony followed a request from the dead serviceman's relatives. It is believed Hauptmann Richard Pahl died in a Brighton Hospital. He was 24 when he was buried with other German servicemen in 1944.

'It is the first time the Brighton branch of the Legion has been asked us to perform a ceremony like this,' said Mr Brook. 'One of our members who was blinded in the war spoke out very strongly that we should honour this request,' said branch chairman Mr Cyril Swannell.

The wreath laid on the carefully tended grave was made by disabled ex-servicemen...

The Evening Argus   20 August 1974.

In the winter of 1940 the Battle of Britain was over but the Luftwaffe continued to harass the British mainland. In June 1943 a new type of aircraft appeared above England, the Messerschmitt Me410, powerful and fast. These aircraft were used, alongside Ju88s, Do217s, He177s, Ju188s and Fw190s on Operation Steinbock, a renewed offensive against London which started as late in the war as the night of 21 January 1944. The most successful attack during this 'Baby Blitz' came on 18 February 1944 when 175 tons of bombs were dropped on London.

One of the units which participated in the Baby Blitz was I/KG51 led by its Kommandeur Hauptmann Unrau and which operated its Messerschmitt Me410s from the airfield at Evreux near St André.

The raids were disastrous for this Gruppe. Two or three crews did not return from each sortie. There were hardly any survivors. A crew that did not return was usually killed. The Mosquito was a formidable opponent and British night-fighter tactics were efficient.

The last attack of the Baby Blitz took place on the night of 18 April 1944. One of the participating pilots was 24-year old Richard Pahl of 1/KG51. Who was Richard Pahl? In 1977 Frau (Mrs) Antonie Gans, Richard Pahl's sister, living in Cologne reminisced:

'Our father was a police official at Ludwigshafen am Rhein, an upright and correct man and our mother a good and very religious woman. Our religious upbringing resulted in us joining the catholic Youth Movement very early. My brother was a catholic youth leader even if this became politically difficult in the middle of the 1930s. But his disarming kindness and his firm appearance meant that he was not really troubled. Anyhow he was pressurised into cooperating with the Hitlerjugend.

'As he had always been fascinated by aviation he decided for the Flieger-HJ (Flying department of the Hitler Youth). He passed his A and B badge at the Gliding Centre at Kirchheim/Teck, and in 1939 he joined the Luftwaffe as a candidate officer. In those times they were still choosy and from 100 candidates 10 at most got through the various examinations.

Below: Highly decorated Oberleutnant Richard Pahl.

'He began his flying schooling at Königsberg and made his first solo flight in January 1940. He became a Leutnant and he was assigned a Junkers Ju88 dive-bomber to operate on the East Front. He received many decorations among others the Deutsches Kreuz in Gold and the *Pokal des Reichsmarschalls für besondere Leistungen im Luftkrieg* (The Reichsmarschall's cup for special accomplishments in the war in the air). But he also was wounded three times. Despite his third and worst injury in 1943, a shot through the lungs, he succeeded at his last gasp to bring back his badly damaged machine (a Ju88) and its crew for a crash-landing at his base, before fainting on the steering wheel.

'The war seemed to be over for him. After many months in hospital, and with the bullet still in his chest, he succeeded in joining his comrades of the Edelweiss Geschwader in northern France even though he had been offered a less dangerous job in the Heimat. In the meantime the fast Me410 bomber had been taken into service and I remember how at one time he said it was a really wild bird but overcomplicated.

'Richard must have had a presentiment of his death, as on 16 April 1944 he wrote a farewell letter to the family. When my brother took over a mission from a comrade and did not return on the night of 18/19 April, he was not the only one who did not come back. The losses had become unbearable and the operation was called to a halt — unfortunately too late for my brother.

'On 20 April 1944 his promotion to Hauptmann, retroactive to 1 April, should have been celebrated. It was done in his absence.

Above: Richard Pahl at the controls of the Junkers Ju88 in which he was severely injured.

Left: A Messerschmitt Me410 being readied for a test flight at Augsburg airfield.

Right: Richard Pahl's wrecked Me410 at Brighton Cemetery.

Indeed Richard Pahl flying Me410 9K+JH, WNr 120005, with his wireless operator Feldwebel Wilhelm Schubert, who had celebrated his 24th birthday only a month before, did not return. They fell victim to the guns of Wg Cdr (now Air Vice-Marshal CB, DSO, DFC, MA, FRAeS) E. D. Crew flying a Mosquito XIII AI Mark VIII, and his Me410 crashed among the tombstones in St Nicholas's churchyard, Brighton.

The Pilot's Individual Report of Wg Cdr E. D. Crew, DFC, of this mission reads as follows:
'Wg Cdr E. D Crew, DFC, (pilot) and WO W. R. Croysdill (operator) took off West Malling at 0010hrs and landed there at 0230hrs. I was patrolling over the Channel at 23,000ft under Wartling GCI (Controller F/C Powell), when I was vectored on to a bogey on a course of 340°.

'Contact was obtained at four miles slightly below and crossing port to starboard on an a/c taking slight evasive action. At full speed the range closed easily and I did not use N2O at all. After four minutes, range was 1,000ft and I obtained an indistinct visual of a twin-engined a/c, which, on closing to 300ft, I believed to be a Ju88. No exhausts were visible. I eased the nose of the Mosquito up and fired a short burst from dead astern, just as the e/a began to dive. This was followed by a last flash from the centre section and cockpit area, and flames.

Above: Richard Pahl's wrecked Me410 at Brighton Cemetery.

Armament report: rounds fired: 20mm SAPI 48
20mm HEI 48

96

Stoppages: Nil
Cine camera exposed 1ft automatically.'

'I followed the a/c down and fired again, with more strikes in the same area, resulting in more white flames and e/a dived very steeply to port. A third deflection burst produced more strikes and flashes and e/a disappeared below me. Visual and contact were lost. I noticed that outboard of each engine there was a cylindrical bulge beneath the wing, resembling the long range tanks of the Fw190. Shortly afterwards I was put on to another contact at 4,000ft height. This e/a was at 3½ miles range, below and to port, flying in a southerly direction. I turned to starboard as it crossed and followed it down through a steep port orbit. Evasive action was moderate and window was being used. As I straightened out of the orbit, an a/c crossed in front at almost collision range, and I had to pull up sharply to avoid hitting it, so that I had no chance to open fire. As it passed below me, I recognised the twin fins and rudders of a Do217. But though I turned round immediately I could not regain contact, and because of the nearness of the French coast I was told to return on 330°.'

'Time of combat 0048. Place of combat R11. At 0050 according to the ROC MG fire was heard at sea, at 055 an a/c later identified as an Me410 crashed in Brighton reference Q72. No ack-ack was heard in the area before 0110, AI 2 (G) report that 20mm cannon strikes have been found on this Me410.

'This a/c was originally claimed as a Ju88 probably destroyed. It is now claimed as an Me410 destroyed in view of the evidence of the British crash.

'Wg Cdr Crew states that his operator said at the time that it was a Me410 but he contradicted him and insisted that it was a Ju88. The inability to see the exhausts from above would also point to its having been, in fact, an Me410.

In 1977 Air Vice-Marshal E. D. Crew, CB, DSO, DFC, MA, FRAes, wrote to the author:
'... Unfortunately I cannot be quite sure of the serial number of the Mosquito, as I see from the log book that I tested a new aircraft on 23 April, but I think it was probably MM499. My aircraft letters were ZJ-V, and the original V was HK426. ZJ, of course, were the squadron letters ...

'At that time we were fitted with nitrous oxide (N₂O) injection to increase the power at altitude, because of such fast targets as the Me410 which were making mini-attacks. This consisted of a large cylinder of the gas, weighing about 500lb, stowed behind the gun bay inside the bomb doors, and a good deal of copper piping round the pilot's side of the cockpit, where there was a tap of the sort you might find in a domestic water system. When turned on one got about three minutes of extra power, so it had to be used at the right moment in a chase. Sometimes when you turned it on the cockpit filled with a kind of snow — if there was a leak somewhere in the system.'

The following day, without disclosing the exact location, the *Brighton and Hove Herald* headlined on its first page: 'NAZI NIGHT RAIDER CRASHES IN CHURCHYARD OF SOUTH COAST TOWN, No Casualties: But Houses Evacuated. Dead Pilot was wearing Iron Cross.

'Believed to have been hit over London, a Messerschmitt fighter-bomber, attempting to return to its base, crashed early on Wednesday morning in a South Coast town; the crippled plane fell in the roadway and crashed through a wall into the churchyard of an ancient and historic church.

Left and above: Photographs of Richard Pahl's burial. These photos were sent to Pahl's family through the services of the International Red Cross, during the war, in 1944.

'The pilot — who was wearing an Iron Cross — was killed, his body being found hanging with his parachute on the branches of a tree on the opposite side of the road...

'The Messerschmitt was returning from Tuesday night's raid on London in which 14 raiders were destroyed...

'The German pilot is understood to have had a shrapnel wound in the head. In addition to the Iron Cross (First Class), he was wearing a medal awarded for service in the Crimea. On the pilot's tunic were also ribbons for other decorations.

Mrs A. Gans:
'The many condolences showed us how loved he was by his comrades and superiors. The Gruppenkommandeur, Hauptmann Murau wrote to my mother: "The loss of our dear Oberleutnant Pahl has deeply shocked all of us, who knew and appreciated him. In your son I lose one of my best Staffelkapitäne, whom we all had taken to heart because of his straightforward and open character. With his death we have lost an officer of whose like they are very few."

'Many months later my mother received, through the International Red Cross his personal belongings and four photographs that had been taken at his burial by the RAF. Three times already we have stood at his grave to adorn it with flowers with our own hands.'

Richard Pahl lies buried at the Heroes Corner, Borough Cemetery, Bear Road, Brighton. His companion on his last flight, Wilhelm Schuberth, whose body was washed ashore on 20 April, lies buried at St James Cemetery, Friston, Eastbourne.

127

The grave of Richard Pahl at Brighton Borough Cemetery. Only one grave of the millions of graves of those killed during World War II.